The Murder
of
Bessie Sheppard

by

David W Marshall

For Lynne and Chris.

Contents

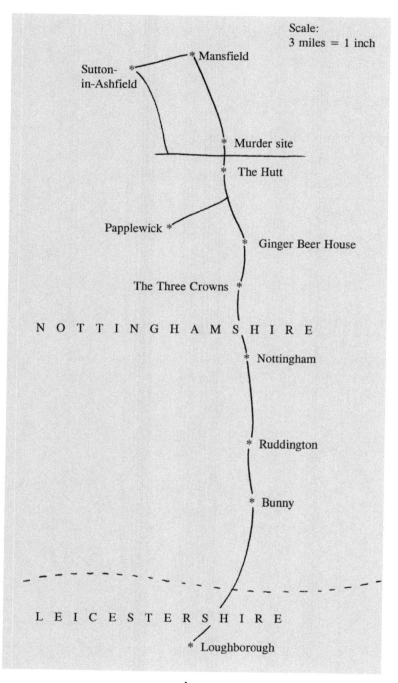

iv

Introduction

It was the summer of 1972. One lunch hour, sandwiches eaten and having nothing better to do with my time, I wandered into Mansfield museum, fully prepared to waste a boring hour gazing aimlessly into glass cases crammed with corroded Roman coins and pre-historic flint axe-heads.

They were there, certainly, but it was something else that caught my eye, something which, unbeknown to me at the time, would set me off on a search that would, in equal parts, both intrigue and frustrate me for the best part of the next forty years of my life. A search that would become an obsession.

It was a news poster. Displayed originally in 1817, it told in lurid detail of the murder of a young woman, Elizabeth Sheppard, and of the execution just three short weeks later, to the day, of her murderer, Charles Rotherham.

The saga of violence sat uncomfortably between the stuffed birds and the papier-mache cross sectional reproductions of the Nottinghamshire coalfield sub-strata. It was, perhaps, this very incongruity that drew me in. The hallowed halls of learning lend uneasy sanctuary to such tales.

I sought out such local history books as I could lay my hands on to learn more. Maybe there were more vicarious thrills to be had. I was disappointed with the distinct lack of information. I had heard of the stone that marked the murder site, just out of town on the main Mansfield to Nottingham trunk road. I passed it frequently. But the books gave very little detail outside of what I had learned at the museum which was, in essence, this:

On the 7th of July, 1817, a seventeen year old girl called Elizabeth Sheppard left her home in the small village of

Papplewick around lunchtime with the intention of travelling to Mansfield to seek work. She was successful in her endeavour and, that evening, while walking home alone, she was brutally beaten to death with a hedgestake. Her shoes and umbrella were stolen from the scene. A man called Charles Rotherham was arrested on the outskirts of Loughborough and, after being found guilty at his trial in Nottingham, was hanged on the 28th of July.

That was it, more or less. My first thoughts were that I found it difficult to reconcile so brief an account with the apparent importance attached to her death by those who thought it necessary to erect a stone in her memory. What was tragedy enough was made all the more appalling by the fact that two people, both of whom had been deprived of life in so violent a manner, were unknown but for the sketchiest of accounts in historical records. If folk had been moved sufficiently in the past to commemorate the event with a substantial stone monument, then surely history owed them at least the token gesture of putting a little flesh on the bones of their memory.

It was no good my bemoaning the lack of detail. The pair had been dead for a century and a half. Maybe there was just nothing more to tell. I wanted to have a look. This is the story of that search....

David Marshall

I.

The Murder
of
Bessie Sheppard

The landscape of 1972 was much changed from that familiar to Bess. The roads then were tree lined and ditched on either side. The boundaries of the town of Mansfield were some two or three miles back from their seventies sprawl.

The A60 road crawls out of Mansfield toward Nottingham sixteen miles away. It soon opens up onto arable farmland before, half a mile further, being overwhelmed by the gloom of the Forestry Commission plantation. It then climbs between sombre lines of dark conifers to the Harlow Wood hospital (now itself long since demolished) and the nationally renowned Portland Training College for the Disabled. Passing beyond the crest of the hill, it descends rapidly southwards to the all but now dry brook known as Rainworth Water.

Traffic is heavy on the A60. Cars roar by oblivious to both the speed restrictions and the stooped warning silhouettes of geriatrics on the road signs. Oblivious, too, to the existence of the stone that lies in the dip, some quarter of a mile below the one-time hospital site, nestling between the hawthorns beside a rough lay-by. It is two feet in height, made of the local red sandstone. Upon the face that overlooks the road is inscribed:

This stone is erected to the memory of Elizabeth Sheppard

of Papplewick who was murdered when passing this spot

by Charles Rotherham, July 7th, 1817.

Around the base of the stone have accumulated discarded crisp bags, Coca-Cola cans - the detritus of modern living that seems the only contribution made of late to her memory. Though no one today seems to cherish her memory, this was clearly not always the case. Soon after her death someone was sufficiently moved to erect a permanent reminder of the murder. And not just that. Oddly the

5

inscription also bore a permanent reminder of the name of her killer.

Bessie Sheppard was no one special, no one famous. She was a girl of supreme irrelevance. So why, I wondered, go to all that trouble?

*　*　*

Mansfield (or Maunsfield as it was in ancient times) is a mining town that straddles the river Maun at the heart of the once great Nottinghamshire coalfield. At the time of my original research it still clung to its mining town identity. Over the ensuing decades its heart was ripped out by dubious political decisions and it became, and to some extent still is, a lost community desperately searching for a new identity.

It is no stranger in modern times to either conflict or strife. In the 1980s it endured the miner's strikes. Internal term interests feuding and the narrow pursuit of short caused the pitmen of Nottinghamshire to break free from their traditional brothers to form the National Union of Democratic Mineworkers. The scars gained in the conflict to a large extent still remain unhealed and the stubborn menfolk of Mansfield, be they right or wrong, remain bloody but unbowed.

Around the central core of the old market town modern Mansfield expands in a great urban complex that once threatened to, and now does, engulf neighbouring towns. Travelling eastward, one passes from Mansfield into the twin pit villages of Forest Town and Clipstone, all but unaware of the transition. Beyond are many purpose-built mining villages that lie in what was once the heart of Sherwood Forest and the Robin Hood country. At its south-western edge Mansfield butts up to the Ashfields - the twin towns of Sutton-in-Ashfield and Kirkby-in-Ashfield. Beyond lies DH Lawrence country.

At the time of my research, in the throes of a prior recession, the only oases of enterprise encountered were the car boot sales and flea markets that emerged to fill whatever space and whatever need arose. Branches of the national chain stores closed with increasing regularity once they realised the bonanza of the miner's redundancy money was drying up. Traditional retailers, long established family firms closed and were replaced by pound discounts and charity shops. Disused premises remained shut, their whitewashed windows staring blindly on to empty streets. Dour faced residents could be seen seeking out second, often third, hand bargains. More often than not they were simply whiling away an hour or two of their abundant time. Unemployment took a heavy toll. In the eyes of the ex-miners there lingered a bitterness, a desolate look that resounded with the fear for their children's futures.

Such a view, at the time, would have caused resentment among the proud folk of Mansfield. But it, and its sister towns, were rapidly degenerating into depressed regions where crime was the only growth industry. Indeed, Mansfield was, for a time, top of the heap for crimes against the person, beating such obvious hotbeds as Glasgow and Merseyside hands down. The rhetoric of politicians fell, and still falls, on deaf ears here. Mansfield people understand only too well the realities of life. It was again, as it had been in the early Nineteenth Century, dying.

***

Back in 1972 my knowledge of Mansfield's history was vague. I knew virtually nothing. It was an ignominious state of ignorance about which I was to grow increasingly ashamed as the years passed. I learned, perhaps wrongly, in school that history was of relevance only within the confines

7

of the classroom amid chalk laden academia. A tedious conglomeration of Palmerstone and Poor Laws, of Disraeli and the Diet of Worms. It existed just for exams. Period. History didn't live. It had nothing to do with me or my life. It took place in some altogether other place.

It was through my research into Bessie Sheppard that I began to notice the changes that were going on around me. I would stare at the vast acreages of retail sprawl that invaded the landscape and realise that I couldn't remember what had been there before, what had been replaced by their glorious transience. New roads punctured the town. Beautiful Victorian terraces were ripped down to service progress. Then, it struck me. This *was* history. I was part of it. I was witnessing both demise and rebirth. The guts and grime of history were here, on my doorstep. Real. Tangible. The panoramas that I had taken for granted were being systematically dismantled, removed from my life as if of no consequence. It was a disquieting experience to suddenly comprehend that I was smack bang in the middle of the programmed destruction of everything I knew.

Given this new perspective I came to understand that if I was witness to so much change in my lifetime, so had it been for Bess and her family. It was clear I could no longer look upon the town, the world even, as being static and dependable. It was dynamic. It was in a state of flux. It was no longer comfortable, nor did it feel safe.

Had Bess felt like this? Had she looked at the world with such dismay? Change can be so remote, so unthreatening, between the covers of a book. Were the early years of the 19th Century any less tortuous for the Sheppards than the last years of the 20th Century and beyond had been for the rest of us? Was, perhaps, the loss of livelihood to the frame knitters with the advent of the broad loom and the power loom not directly paralleled by the loss of the pits to the miners? The march of progress was inexorable. The casualties were immense. Its direction and purpose, suspect.

I had a clapped out mini in the early seventies. Grass green with a black hand-painted roof in which the brush strokes were visible. The windscreen wipers jammed continually and I'd frequently have to lean out of the window to coax them back to life. The heater, not to be outdone, had given up the ghost at the first signs of frost, so my early morning journeys to Nottingham, where I then worked, were accomplished only with a brace of hot water bottles, one perched on the dashboard to act as a rudimentary de-icer, the other clamped tightly between my thighs serving a much more crucial purpose. It was thus ill-equipped that I made my first trip to Papplewick in the closing months of 1972 to finds Bess' origins.

***

Papplewick is a small village that lies to the west of the main A60, south of Mansfield itself by some seven miles and close to Newstead Abbey, the beautiful, but crumbling, one time home of Lord Byron. Byron left in 1816, before our story begins, troubled by accusations of sodomy and incest. The village itself lies upon a crossroad, strung out in linear fashion along the arms of the intersecting roads. To the north and east these roads meet the A60, to the south lies the Bestwood suburb of Nottingham and the city itself.

At the centre of Papplewick stands the Griffin's Head, a family pub with swings, pub food, guest ales and sporting a playing field where on warm summer evenings, as if sealed in a time warp, many a game of family cricket is enjoyed. The River Leen runs down from the Newstead estate, bisecting the village, before going on to join the Trent in Nottingham.

It took me little time to look around Papplewick, still less to fall under its spell. Welcoming stone cottages now fetch a high price on today's market, yet the tranquillity of the place is scarcely disturbed in its cosy rural landscape. With Nottingham close by and the main M1 artery but a stone's throw away, it's an idyllic, but costly, place to live.

A parish church dedicated to St. James has stood on the site just north of the village centre since Norman times, but the current building was stepped back in time. Fanciful though it may seem, it seems to resonate with the souls of those long gone, you can all but hear the shuffling feet of the crocodiles of black-decked only constructed as recently as 1795 by the local Montagu family. Built of a rich, honeyed stone it stands at the end of a single track lane at the northern end of the village. Double iron gates open onto an even narrower tree-lined approach that slopes gently down to meet the churchyard proper. Popular legend suggests the grave of Robin Hood's roving minstrel, Alan-a-Dale, lies here, but then many similar such claims are made for other members of his Merrie Men in local parishes. It's impossible to wander down this lane and not experience the sensation of having mourners winding their way down over the centuries to pay last respects to family and friends.

Before the main door to the church stands an ancient yew whose contorted limbs furnished, in days long gone, the wood for the archer's bows. Its boughs hang heavy with age, forming a canopy beneath which visitors can linger, resting on the circular bench that surrounds the gnarled girth of its impressive trunk.

The graves here span some three hundred years, from the late sixteen hundreds to the present day. On this, my first visit, I did little more than savour its tranquillity. In a way, it was a place you could almost enjoy being dead.

***

10

The slog through local histories proved fruitless. The many photographs of old Mansfield, though, were splendidly evocative, showing gritty, determined residents. Their dourness, I suspected, owed less to the personality of the folk depicted and rather more to the requirements of the exposure times necessary to capture the image.

In these same books Bess warranted barely a mention. Though overflowing with a wealth of detail regarding the names of churchwardens and the incumbents of a myriad municipal posts, they did not bring the place to life. Of the little I did learn in school, England, and by extension, Mansfield, was a dire place in which to live - let alone be poor - in the 19th Century. It was this that seemed to be missing. That the last thing to record for posterity was the fact the Mansfield, too, was a place of poverty and degradation.

But then, who was I to rock the boat? A young upstart whose only qualification for comment was a finely nurtured ignorance of all around me capped off with a barely scraped History 'O' level. Was I up to it? Or was there a different tale to tell? And, if so, what the hell was it?

Despite the insecurity I decided to start with contemporaneous writings in the press. The local Mansfield papers didn't go back far enough, but a phone call to the Evening Post in Nottingham established that they had records dating back as far as I needed and yes, they would be more than happy to grant me access. I made an appointment with the archivist for the following day, then phoned in sick to work.

The Evening Post offices then stood in the centre of the city just across from the Theatre Royal. I entered the three storey building rather like a child tentatively boarding a ghost train - scared, but excited. The receptionist wrote down my name, eyeing the Bob Dylan tee shirt I wore which announced to the world that I would no longer work on Maggie's farm, and picked up the internal phone.

"Mr Marshall's here," she said, her pleasant smile only serving to underline my sense of inadequacy.

The archivist appeared. A small man with a wispy crest of thin white hair, wearing a navy pinstripe suit, he had a manner that gave meaning to the word dapper. He could easily have stepped from the pages of a Dickens' novel. He led me slowly through a labyrinth of corridors, up endless, narrow, lung-splitting staircases until we emerged, light headed, on the uppermost floor of the building where he showed me into a long, railway carriage like room, whose flaking window sills looked over into the bowels of a grubby inner courtyard. He had said not one word to me on our journey, but now, to which period I was interested in. 1817, I told him.

"Ah," he said, "the Regency."

He left the room, returning shortly afterwards, his frail body unbowed by the unwieldy bulk of massive broadsheet ledgers which he lovingly placed before me on the inclined reading surface which ran the full length of one wall.

"There you are, sir," he said. "I'll leave you to it. I'm in the end vestibule should you need assistance."

Wholly disarmed by his polite deference, I thanked him, certain that it was I who should address him as 'sir', not vice versa. It was his territory. Did he resent me in any way? He certainly showed no signs. Maybe, like a mother proudly showing off her infant, he was grateful for any interest shown in his offspring. I hoped so.

For a long moment I sat staring at the impressive ledgers. The heavily hand-tooled leather binders, ingrained with countless decades of dust, were redolent of a time when things mattered more. It felt like an adventure and I would doubtless have savoured it more had I been aware at the time that never again would I lay my hands on the real thing. The next time I would explore them, their content would be safely - and sensibly - ensconced upon microfiche in the local library. There was a sense of real privilege, a belief that I was actually also touching the history I was reading. The ivory hue of the pages demanded delicacy. Though seemingly fragile beyond belief, they were, in reality, a good deal more robust than I gave them credit for, though I was capable of doing them immense harm. Every contact with humans takes its toll. The minute traces of acid in perspiration, when transferred from the fingers, would attack the paper. Air pollution would prematurely age it. Proximity to such documents made me acutely aware of the need to preserve them for future generations, just as those already departed had done for me. It wasn't enough that they should survive just this long, I wanted them around for good. If that meant them being consigned to microfiche or held on computer files, so be it.

The binders contained copies of both the Nottingham Review and the Nottingham Journal. Both sets of documents dated from the early 19th Century. Each individual page was covered by its own protective tissue. I approached July of 1817 like a child who had saved his best sweet for last. The print was small, uneven, difficult to decipher, especially in the fading afternoon light. I screwed up my eyes. Then, there it was. No headline, just a first word in upper case beginning the story.

"HORRIBLE murder....", it began.

So great was my excitement I don't to this day believe I actually read anything then or that it registered with me. There was little time left. The afternoon was wearing on and I had a bus to catch (this being yet another occasion that my car was in dock). I set about the arduous task of robotically

13

copying the article into my notebook. Whatever other secrets the ledgers held would have to wait.

I travelled home in a daze, imagining myself variously as detective, historian, adventurer, seeker of truth. I was Indiana Jones even before he'd been invented, of that there was no doubt. Later, settling myself down in a dark corner of my local I began to sample the fruits of my search.....

"HORRIBLE murder - On Tuesday last the body of a young woman was found in the ditch near Rainworth Water in the parish of Sutton-in-Ashfield, in this county and about a mile distant from the toll bar on the turnpike road leading from Mansfield to Nottingham. It proved to be that of Elizabeth Sheppard, an interesting girl about 17 or 18 years of age, and the daughter of a woman residing at Papplewick, who had left home the preceding day for Mansfield to enquire after some work, and having succeeded in her mission was on her return home in the evening alone. It is supposed that she had been waylaid or overtaken by some ruffian who, with a heavy bludgeon or some other such like weapon did batter her about the head and other parts of the body until she was dead, and then threw her in the ditch after taking from her person a pair of shoes and her umbrella. Her head presented a most shocking spectacle, being so disfigured, that her features could scarcely be recognised; the brains protruding from the skull and one eye completely knocked from its socket and lay upon her cheek. Some quarrymen on going to work the next morning near the spot observed some halfpence lying on the ground, which induced them to look further, when to their astonishment and horror the mangled body met their sight; through the hedge lying as above described. A gentleman and a lady who happened to be travelling by in a gig shortly afterwards and saw the body gave information of the circumstances at the police office in this town, immediately on their arrival and the most effective steps were instantly taken to trace out and secure

14

the murderer. *From the disordered state of the young creature's dress, when found, there is reason to conclude that her assailant had made some attempt upon her chastity, and it is not improbable, that the efforts she made to resist him had aroused the fury of the wretch and determined him instantly to deprive her of life. Near the spot where the body was discovered, a stick or hedgestake has since been found, besmeared with blood which is believed to be the instrument with which the murderer's deed was perpetrated. The body was removed to Sutton where a Coroner's Inquest has been sitting these two days.*

From other particulars which have transpired it would appear that the unhappy mother was fated to meet the ruthless murderer of her hapless child, on the public highway soon after the horrid deed had been committed and not more than half a mile from the place. Feeling an anxious desire for the young woman's return she went out towards the evening to meet her when a man passed her on the way, with an umbrella under his arm, who, from various corroborative circumstances there is reason to presume was the identical murderer. On the next day when the intelligence was communicated of the fatal catastrophe which had befallen the girl, it had such effect on the mother's feelings as to throw her into fits and her mind has ever since continued in a state of frenzy. No time was lost by the police in making the most diligent search for the ruffian, and it was soon ascertained that he had slept at the Three Crowns Red Hill on Monday night where he had disposed of a pair of woman's shoes and that he had previously offered the same for sale at the Ginger Beer House near the 7th mile stone. From Red Hill he was traced on the road to Loughborough and was subsequently apprehended by two Nottingham constables having sold the umbrella at the Rancliffe Arms, Bunny. He says his name is Wm. Rotherham, that he is a native of Sheffield and by trade a scissor grinder. On examining his clothes stains of blood appeared in several places. He was conveyed heavily ironed to Sutton, for examination, and it is expected will be fully committed for trial this day dawned. After the perpetration of the murder the ruffian called at the Hutt with an acquaintance, a soldier whom he accidentally met with, and the latter has been detained for examination."

The date at the head of this edition of the Nottingham Journal was the 14th of July, just seven days after the murder. Such was the wealth of new material it contained I had difficulty absorbing it. Indeed, with so much information amassed so quickly, I began to wonder with regard to its veracity. How accurate was it? By 1972 the depths to which the tabloid press would eventually sink had been by no means reached, yet it seemed from this report that, even back then, the seeds had been demonstrated to have been sown.

Despite my tenuous grasp of history, I was fairly confident that law enforcement in 19th Century England did not boast within its array of available techniques either fingerprints, efficient communications, psychological profiling or the internal combustion engine. That being the case, how were they able to arrest Rotherham so soon after the murder and so far from the scene? I needed more reports of events to make comparisons. I also needed to vastly increase my knowledge of the workings of the infant police force.

By far the most poignant information in the article was the suggestion of the mother's chance meeting with the killer of her daughter. What truth was there in this? If, as the article implied, he had been carrying Bess' umbrella, why did she not recognise it? Where did they pass? Had she been *thrown into fits*, how reliable would her replies be to the Regency equivalent of Piers Morgan? Assuming, that is, that questions were ever really put.

There were so many questions raised by the report that highlighted gaps in my own knowledge. I had naively believed that once I had my hands on a reliable account of the events of July 1817, my questions would be answered. In reality, they had multiplied.

**

It was imperative I obtain an accurate picture of the geography of both the murder site and the greater area of his pursuit. I began locally. Dame Fortune has never been a reliable companion but, on this occasion, she gave a cursory nod in my direction. For years it had been my habit to visit the library on Saturday mornings after stocking up with fruit and vegetables for the family for the week at the nearby market. On this fortuitous occasion I was upstairs in the reference room when, quite by chance, my attention was drawn to a map that for many years hung on the wall. It was some eight feet square and was covered by thick, protective plastic. Kneeling at its foot I examined the flourish of script in its bottom corner. It was a map of Nottinghamshire, but better still, it dated from the first two decades of the 19th Century. Careful examination revealed the location of the main Nottingham toll roads, the access roads to Papplewick in use then, even the site of the toll bars. Everything I needed.

The route of the present Nottingham Road appears to tally almost exactly with the old road depicted. The milestones were individually marked and, at the seventh, mentioned in the Journal report, was shown the location of the old Ginger Beer House where Rotherham is said to have stopped. I knew it in 1972 as a small restaurant. I did not know where in the village of Papplewick Bess had lived, so had to guess the route her mother might have taken when she went to look for her. It seemed likely to have been along what we now know as Blidworth Waye. There was an alternative, an old coach road that cut through the grounds

17

of Newstead Abbey, but, had she walked that way it seemed unlikely to afford any passing place for her and Charles Rotherham except exactly at the toll bar itself.

The article alleged that, after the crime, Rotherham went drinking in The Hutt. The Hutt, though much aggrandised, still exists today, opposite the main gates to Newstead Park on the main road to Nottingham between the toll bar and the side road to Papplewick from which Bess' mother seems likely to have emerged. The two must have passed, were the reports to be believed, somewhere between The Hutt and the toll bar, which then stood on a crossroad, equidistant between the murder site and the Papplewick turning.

It was a relief to find the topography so little changed from Bess' day and that I could, in the main, rely upon modern maps in my enquiries.

***

To begin with the detective work was fine. I was having fun beginning to piece together the events of July 7th 1817. But the crunch, I knew, was coming. Vast gaps in my knowledge of 19th Century England had to be filled. That meant history books and, having painstakingly perfected my aversion to them in school, this was not to be a labour filled with too much love. The only sensible way to proceed was in piecemeal fashion, bit by plodding bit. Though I would never advocate such an approach to any serious student working to a deadline, it worked fine for me. I could dabble here and there then, before terminal ennui set in, I could make my escape back to the old records. The drawback was that progress was slow and, for long periods where the rest of my life intervened, non-existent. Things which should have slotted into place instantly simply didn't. I had to backtrack frequently, cross-refer and regroup the wagons constantly before the obvious significance of things struck

18

me. It was a long, slow process, but its very slowness flattened my learning curve.

What had initially drawn me to the quest was the people, the characters in the story and their place in the landscape of 1817. This landscape, crucial and fascinating though it ultimately proved to be, was of secondary importance in the early days. I was slipping into history by the back door and there would be those who would criticise any conclusions I might reach for that reason alone. My only response was that any door was better than no door at all and, were it not for back door tactics, there might be many areas of life in which understanding was curtailed by the preciousness of experts.

There is a technique long used by archaeologists and police alike, whereby, with a deep understanding of musculature and the study of a skull's contours, it's possible to reconstruct the face it once bore. In crime investigation missing people have been located, in archaeology we have come face to face with Richard III in the Leicester car park. Quite how rigorous the procedure is, quite where the scientist relinquishes control to the artist, I don't know. Where does interpretation take over from irrefutable fact? I ask these questions only to emphasise the nature of the task I felt was at hand. History is a discipline within which the historian must exercise restraint. He must use his knowledge and intelligence - tempered by his own humanity - to put flesh on the cold facts without in anyway knowingly compromising the integrity of the whole. It is the historian's responsibility to use received wisdom in the reconstruction of real human lives, real experience. He must steer clear of tangential flights of fancy and confine himself to the probable with but infrequent detours into the possible.

Thus armed with my makeshift philosophy I took my first tentative steps into the world of early England with a look at the system of law and order.

19

We take the police force today for granted. Respect or distrust them, they are a part of life. But, for the vast majority of Britain at the opening of the 19th Century, the police did not exist. Not, that is, in any form that would have effectively deterred prospective wrongdoers. Though the larger cities did have something resembling a fledgling police force, the smaller towns and villages made do with local enforcement officers, the recruitment of whom was organised on a parish by parish basis. These were the parish constables. They were volunteers, unpaid except for a small contribution to their travelling expenses. They had other jobs too. Blacksmith, farmer - anyone fit and willing would do. They had no equipment, wore no uniforms and were wholly untrained. They were appointed by the Justices of the Peace. JPs were drawn from among the ranks of local dignitaries, were of good character and, not unusually, wealthy too. They were responsible for the organisation of the local road tolls, arranged the collection of taxes and generally oversaw the day to day business in the county.

By the time of the murder of Bessie Sheppard the cities and some of the larger towns had a rudimentary organised constabulary. The expertise of such a force, however, was not great, for the men employed at the outset were the very same who served earlier as volunteers. To imagine the new force could execute any quantum leap in law enforcement would be wrong.

Conditions in the country, however, demanded the formation of a full time force for law and order. Civil unrest was rife. The advent of mechanisation in the textile industry and the consequent loss of income to the many framework knitters, coupled with the high prices demanded for basic commodities sparked off riots, notably the Luddite uprisings of Lancashire, Yorkshire and the Midlands. Their emergence has always been linked with the introduction of the power loom, but it was inextricably linked to the general state of decline in the land. Without any organised force the bulk of responsibility for dealing with these disturbances fell to the military, but the military was otherwise engaged. We were at war with Napoleon. A civilian force was essential.

Today, through the media, we are familiar with modern policing methods, and this familiarity makes it difficult to understand how the force in the early 1800s could function at all. There was no forensic science. Fingerprinting didn't exist. There were few, if any, rules of evidence. No protection existed for the accused person and no legal aid system was in place to provide a defence. Indeed, before 1836 there was no statutory role for defence counsel and no right of cross examination of witnesses whatever. In short, you spoke for yourself, then they hanged you. The strongest possible evidence that could be laid before the court was that of confession. Today, such evidence in isolation would normally be insufficient to secure a conviction. Corroborative evidence, be it forensic or circumstantial, would be needed in support. It would, however, be unfair to judge the judicial system of the time by present standards. Hindsight is a luxury too often employed to condemn the past in the arrogant belief that now, in what we consider to be more enlightened times, we occupy some higher moral ground. In 1817, if a man confessed to murder, it was enough to justify his hanging. They may have been frequently wrong in their judgement, but it was the best they had.

*** *** ***

When I visited the murder site in the middle of 1973 it was a year since I had been in the museum. Why I had returned I can't remember, but I was frequently drawn there. In a month it was to be the 156th anniversary of the murder. Maybe by being there on that day I would feel some sense of Bess and her killer. Though a convinced atheist and

21

having no truck with the supernatural I was aware that some of its supporters held a rather quasi-scientific theory in which the very fabric of reality could act almost as a recording medium, absorbing the molecular impact of events long gone by. Thus, they accounted for ghosts. Matter flung into playback.

Despite both my scepticism and the fact that the location, beside the main road, hardly seemed conducive to some pseudo-romantic manifestation of a murdered innocent, I did wonder if the presence of someone who cared could make a difference. The human brain, the imagination, is capable of much. Was it simply imagination or did the place call to me, desperate to divulge some long held secret? I wandered through the undergrowth surrounding the stone. Branches of infant birches whispered above my head. I could not dispel the thought that this was where it happened. No matter what physical changes had taken place - they were superficial - the very soil beneath my feet was that upon which Bess lay dead all those years before.

It was much later I heard the stories of the ghost. Though they never did convert me, rumour has it that, were the stone ever to move, she would appear. Where the origins of this story lay I never did discover, (there were rumours of a spectral manifestation after a car hit the stone, but I found it odd Bess should wait for the invention of the internal combustion engine before appearing) but there are people who believe she has been seen. The most recent sighting back then was in 1967 when an ambulance driver, John Lindley, was on his way home from Nottingham after a night shift in the early hours of the morning. As he passed the stone the figure of a young girl, clad in white, stood in the dip by the roadside. I have no reason to doubt John Lindley's story, nor do I have any other explanation for it. It's just another chapter in the legend. The place does have a certain eeriness, the source of which may well lie in the mind.

***

I was disappointed when next I rang the press to discover that they were now reluctant to grant me access to their archive, advising me that, for reasons of conservation, they preferred I use the microfiche copies available in the main public library in Nottingham on Angel Row. Available turned out to be something of a euphemism.

The thoroughfare known as Angel Row has little to do with cherubic reality. It's situated in the centre of the city, just off the main city square, affectionately known locally as Slab Square. Then it was surrounded by shops, pubs, a large cinema and strangled by throngs of pedestrians. The frontage of the library owed all to 1960s Soviet supermarket style, resembling in no way a repository of learning. Rising above the bustle, it served the people of Nottingham well.

The records I needed, though technically available, were by no means readily accessible unless one was to arrive at the crack of dawn and take a vanguard place in the queue, hoping against hope that no more than a couple of bewildered pensioners out of the city's half million folk had harboured similar desires. After a considerable wait I finally secured a microfiche reader and found what I was after, a record of the murder that pre-dated the previous one that had been published in the Nottingham Review of July 11th 1817. It read:

"Murder is a crime happily but of rare occurrence in this country, and when a deed of this dark description has been committed, every feeling of the human heart rises up, anxious to discover the perpetrator of such a dreadful outrage, and the mind cannot rest satisfied, till the murderer has been delivered into the hands of justice. Murder carries

with it such an appalling sound, such dreadful ideas, that human nature starts back affrighted, and is shocked at the contemplation of the horrid deed. It is not only a crime against the law of the land, but a crime against the law of God and the laws of nature, and therefore every man is anxious for its punishment. Sorry we are to say that our calendar will at the approaching assize be stained by a crime of this odious description.

On Monday last, an interesting young woman of the name Elizabeth Sheppard, about eighteen years of age, and who bore an excellent character, being out of work, determined upon going to Mansfield to seek employment, and having succeeded in the object of her errand, was returning home to inform her friends, when near the third milestone, on the Mansfield road, she was accosted and attacked by a ruffian, who it is supposed grossly insulted her, by beating her about the head and body with a large hedgestake. In the course of the evening she was discovered lying in the ditch adjoining Rainworth Water, near the toll bar on the road to Mansfield. Her head was bruised in a shocking manner, one of her eyes being knocked out, and her brains scattered about in all directions.

The body was removed to the Unicorn in Sutton-in-Ashfield, and a coroner's inquest sat on Wednesday, but no verdict was pronounced, the proceedings being adjourned to this day, principally on account of the impracticability of getting witnesses from such different and distant quarters.

Information of the murder was immediately sent to Nottingham, and by the active exertions of our excellent police, suspicion fell upon a man of the name of Charles Rotherham, a native of Sheffield, by trade a scissor grinder.

This man had slept at Red Hill, and left the shoes at the Three Crowns, in that place; he went through Nottingham about ten in the morning, inquiring his way to

24

Loughborough and sold the umbrella before he arrived at that place. Barnes and Lingegar, two of our most active officers were dispatched on horseback to Loughborough and traced him on the way, and when about a half a mile on this side of that place they came up with him and instantly recognised him by the description which had been given them. They instantly secured him, and also a young man who was in his company, but against whom, we understand, there is not likely to be anything substantiated. They were brought into Nottingham on Monday night and lodged in the county gaol. Rotherham's clothes were spotted with blood, and since his arrest he has confessed to the perpetration of the horrid deed. We understand he has a wife but no children; he is about forty five years of age, and stands five feet one inches high.

Yesterday the unfortunate girl was interred in Papplewick churchyard, followed by her weeping relatives and a large body of spectators. The singers belonging to a dissenting congregation at Hucknall (a village in the neighbourhood) were invited to attend at her mother's house, next to Robinson's Mill, they accordingly went and sung a hymn over the corpse at the door; they also followed to church, and sung as the procession went through the town. The minister of the place was informed by note, that it was the wish of her friends that a hymn should be sung over the grave, and as no answer was returned, it was naturally conceived that silence gave consent, accordingly, after the ritual of the church had been gone through, and before the grave was filled up, one of the singers began to give out that beautiful hymn of Dr. Watts beginning:

When blooming youth is snatched away...

but Mr H, the minister, interfered and in a manner not very much to the credit of the CLOTH, would not allow them to proceed, but peremptorily told them to go about their business, using language which our informant terms

25

abusive. We apprehend such conduct as this will not exalt him in the opinion of his parishioners neither will it at all contribute to lessen the number of dissenters.

Here was new information. Bess had been taken to the Unicorn in Sutton-in-Ashfield. It sounded like a pub though, despite my considerable knowledge of the town, not one of which I had ever heard. There were also several material differences between the two reports. One gives his name as William Rotherham, the other Charles. The Review had said that Bess' body had been found on the Monday evening, the same day as the murder, whereas the Journal reported that she had been discovered by quarrymen on their way to work in the early hours of Tuesday, the day following the murder. If, as the Review stated, Rotherham had slept at the Three Crowns in Red Hill (still on the Mansfield side of Nottingham city) and then passed through Nottingham at ten in the morning, it made it unlikely he could have also been transported back to Nottingham the same day. He was on foot. His pursuers on horseback and presumably questioning many people en route. The Journal I concluded, had to be right. The body of Bess was found on the Tuesday morning.

With the funeral taking place on Thursday July 10th and being reported, in some detail, in the Review of the 11th, it seemed hardly surprising that some of the supposed facts were somewhat suspect. Even with modern technology to meet tight deadlines the press are not strangers to a certain creativity.

By far the most intriguing part of the Review's account (and one which, from the abrupt change of style in the language, may well have been tacked on as an afterthought by a different author) were the bizarre events at the funeral. I resolved to add to the list of 'things I didn't actually know a whole lot about', a note to research the set up for 19th Century organised religion.

For now though, the search was on to find Bess' home and grave. The Review told me she lay in Papplewick churchyard and, while not actually divulging her door number, did at least have a sprinkling of clues as to where I might start looking.

***

It was now Springtime. I stood once more in Papplewick churchyard. The sun was slipping low behind the trees in the early evening sky, washing the honeyed stone of the church with a soft, golden light. Most of the graveyard was kept neat and well tended, but there were areas that were tragically overgrown, particularly to the right and the rear of the church itself. Though a simple task to locate graves contemporary with Bess, her own resting place eluded me. I proceeded into the jungle. Many of the memorials in these areas had been erected facing the prevailing wind and had, consequently, had such inscriptions as they once had blasted from their soft sandstone surface. I persevered for a while, but emerged eventually from the tangle of waist high grass and nettles, disappointed. Only then, sweating and bedraggled, did it occur to me that the chances of there actually being a gravestone were minimal. Bess had been seeking work when she was killed. The family were poor. Why should I expect to find a gravestone? I had been in many graveyards before and had been struck by the dearth of even basic headstones for long stretches of the past, when every penny earned had to go to putting bread on the table, food in the bellies of the kids. It was a disappointing proposition, but maybe there just would be no sign of her grave. And yet, wasn't it paradoxical that there should be no monument to her here, where she lay beneath the ground, yet where she died, at the scene of her murder, there should be so substantial a memorial? Surely whatever sentiment had been responsible for the erection of the stone would have ensured some marker for this, her final resting place?

27

I was on the point of leaving when, leaning against a rusting fence beside the steps down to the oak door of a small but functional looking storage room, I noticed a small rectangle of slate, barely eight inches by twelve. Upon its face, coarsely chiselled, was the meagre legend,

ELIZABETH

SHEPPARD

1800 - 1817

There have been few times in my life when I have seen anything so simple yet so moving. This was no memorial of great distinction. It was crude, done by someone local; perhaps someone who knew her. Though initially taken aback by the roughness of the carved letters and the way it just rested against the railing, out of sight in an isolated corner of the graveyard, I soon grew to feel how much more appropriate was its simplicity, so unlike the other at the site of her death. A vast gulf separated the two. This was placed with love. The other, I began to suspect, may have been to serve a wholly different purpose.

***

Having been unable, as yet, to discover the whereabouts of Bess' home, I turned my attention to the furore that erupted at her funeral. Just who was Mr H, the minister, and what was it that had so annoyed him? I returned to the library and began once more to plough through the records. There, this time in the Nottingham Journal of July 19th 1817, was the following letter from the very same Mr H, addressed to the editor of the paper. It read,

Sir, I have just now seen a paragraph in the Nottingham Review of last week, containing some remarks upon my conduct as Minister of Papplewick, at the interment of Elizabeth Sheppard, on Thursday last (the unfortunate

young woman who was found murdered near Rainworth Water). If the Editor of that paper values his integrity, he will not hesitate either to correct so gross a mis-statement of facts, as he there relates, or give up the name of his informant.

No note expressing a wish that a hymn should be sung over the grave, was ever received by me - nor any other note, except the one of which I have subjoined a copy; the original I have enclosed to you, which was delivered into my hands about noon on that day, by a person, who said he brought it from Mary Sheppard. Nor was any other application made to me on this distressing occasion for permission to sing. Whenever a wish has been signified to me by friends or relatives of a deceased person, to have a psalm, or any other part of the funeral service sung I have ever most readily acquiesced.

As far as I have been able to ascertain, the distressed mother of this unfortunate young woman was almost in a state of insensibility and distraction, and incapable of giving any directions relating to the funeral of her daughter. No-one more truly sympathised with her than I did, knowing her to be a very respectable character.

No abusive language was used by me, as the congregation assembled can testify; but I expressed my honest indignation at singers belonging to a dissenting congregation atHucknall impertinently intruding themselves on my official duties in Papplewick churchyard, and as the informant of this part of his narrative correctly states, I desired them to go about their business. The words given out for the purposes of singing or preaching I did not distinctly hear; but I had reason to believe they formed no part of the church burial service - and as such I had no authority to permit them to be used.

I avail myself of the medium of your Journal, to assure the Editor of the Review and his informant, that I have the approbation of all those of my parishioners, whose opinion I value, for my conduct on this occasion; and I have too great a respect for every conscientious Dissenter, to believe, that the number will be increased by this intemperate and injudicious zeal.

I am Sir your constant reader and obedient servant,

Thos. Hurt Junr. Curate of Papplewick/Linby.

17th July 1817.

The footnote to which he referred in his letter read:

Sir - Mary Sheppard will be glad if you will send word by the bearer, what time it will be convenient to bury her daughter this afternoon.

M. Sheppard

The letter angered me. Wasn't it enough that Bess had been killed without she become a pawn in the petty politics of religion? Nothing in Hurt's letter convinced me that the vicar had any real concern for Bess and her family. There was much there, however, that pointed to his wounded pride. The note from Mary Sheppard asking when it would be *convenient* to bury her daughter was heart-breaking. And the fiasco didn't end there. Ever true to its conviction that it was the voice of the people, the Review printed a rebuttal to Hurt in its edition of July 25th. It read,

To the editor of the Nottingham Review.

Sir - As the curate of Papplewick has in the Nottingham Journal of last week publically called on you to either correct what he calls there a 'gross mis-statement of facts', published in the Review a fortnight ago, relative to his

shameful conduct at the interment of the unfortunate young woman who was found murdered at Rainworth Water; or give up the name of your informant. We feel it is our duty to come forward and voluntarily answer for ourselves; and we think this the more necessary as Mr H not only at the churchyard, in his 'honest indignation' was pleased to call us an impertinent, busy, meddling set, intruding upon his official duties but he would hint to the public through the medium of the Journal, that through our intemperate or injudicial zeal we intruded ourselves upon the friends of the deceased in order to preach and sing as he terms it; for he says the mother was not capable of giving any directions about the funeral. If this be true we must have attended without her invitation; but the following circumstances will show he was mistaken; she attended the corpse to the grave, which is a distance of more than a mile and there Mr H manifested how tenderly he could sympathise with her in her distress. It is not our intention to render evil for evil, or railing for railing, but we will lay before you, Sir, and the public, a clear account of the affair from first to last, and let the facts speak for themselves.

The unfortunate girl having been a scholar in our Sunday School, and acquainted with many of our singers, we received an invitation to attend the funeral and sing a hymn over the grave. After some consideration the request was complied with, and we went to the house. Before we attempted to sing at all, we were informed by some friends of the deceased, that a note had been sent to the minister, expressing a wish that a hymn might be sung over the grave, but no answer was returned; we therefore concluded that he had no objection. This was the ground on which we proceeded. We sang a hymn at the door, and as the procession moved through the town; but having arrived at the grave and Mr H having finished reading the burial service, and turned his back to go into the church, one of the singers gave out two lines of the hymn as mentioned in the

31

Review; when to our astonishment the same fountain that had just been yielding sweet waters, began to cast forth bitter.

The following are some of the expressions made use of by Mr H in giving vent to his 'honest indignation' - whether they are abusive or not, we leave to everyone to judge. Turning himself about and coming towards us, he began; I don't allow such proceedings as these; I am the authorised minister of the place; I have performed the service appointed for the occasion, and I will have none of your singing and preaching here, you are impertinent, a busy meddling set, go about your business. What business have you here? The person who was giving out the hymn immediately shut the book and bowing to Mr H answered, very well, Sir, and offered to make an apology, but Mr H proceeded in such a hasty manner, that the person was some time before he could be heard, at length, however, he answered, we did not come here of our own accord, we were requested to attend. Mr H answered, I did not send for you, you are a shabby, impudent, intruding set of people, go about your business; I am sorry to disturb the congregation by being put in such a passion. There is no occasion for passion said the person, but there is, said Mr H, it is like the rest of your impertinence, going about the country noising and bawling. Sir, said one of the singers, you have given us permission before to sing in your churchyard. I never did answered Mr H. The person replied, I was one of the persons that asked you leave. Mr H rejoined, you had the impudence to sing before without my permission; and much more to the same import, which we do not think it necessary to insert - this being sufficient specimen of the language made use of by him, on this occasion.

This Sir, is to the best of our knowledge, a faithful account of the business; and we trust, in giving it, we have not been influenced by that bigotry, or party spirit, that intemperate or injudicious zeal which caused Mr H so injudiciously to expose himself in Papplewick churchyard. If he conceived it was a spirit of opposition that urged us to sing or preach as he terms it, he is greatly mistaken. It was we trust, from motives far different, and in that spirit of Christian love that envieth not, vaunteth not itself, is not puffed up, doth not behove itself unseemly, seeketh not her own, is not easily provoked, thinketh no evil etc. And whatever authority Mr H may have, until he becomes possessed of this spirit he is but as sounding brass and tinkling cymbal.

We remain Sir yours etc.

George Allen, Joseph King, Hugh Wright, John Piggin, William Meadows, George Goodall, William Thumbs.

Editor - We have seen the writer of the note since, and she says, she was desired to mention it in the note, but she omitted it. Mr H is therefore correct in this particular. He had nevertheless been asked leave on a former occasion by two of our singers and he had readily acquiesced but which he readily denied when told of it on this occasion.

There, thankfully, the battle in the newspapers ceased and both factions returned to their states of mutual disrespect. My enquiries revealed that the Hurt family was no stranger to the cloth. Thomas Jnr's father, again Thomas Hurt, had been rector of Sutton-in-Ashfield from 1774 to his death in 1820. Thomas Jnr was born in 1773, just before his father took up pastoral duties for that parish. At the time of Bess' funeral Thomas Hurt was a married man of 44.

The late 18th and early 19th Centuries were contentious times for organised religion. Part of the trouble seemed to have been due to the emergence of the non-conformist chapels. Wesleyan Methodism has strong roots here. With the dissenters came, understandably enough, the dissenting dissenters. One of these hybrid offshoots was the Methodist New Connexion. They founded a chapel in the nearby town of Hucknall (wherein stands the church to which in 1824 the body of the poet Byron was to be returned). Here they became, not complementary to Thomas Hurt's Christianity, but competition. It was their Sunday School that Bess attended - and here was yet another reason for the bad blood between the faiths.

The Established Church decided that the Sunday Schools acted contrary to the will of God. In the early 19th Century they taught the young, and the not so young, not just the scriptures, but to read, write and, as they put it, sum. To teach on a Sunday was contrary to God's will. There was, however, more to it than that.

Educational standards in England were appalling. Across the country dissent was rife. Poverty, disease and hunger were commonplace. The government chose to sit back and watch. It suited them, as is so often the case, to keep the population in a blissful state of ignorance. Luddism, with its violence and rebellion, was in full cry. A populace maintained in ignorance was less of a threat than one that was adequately educated. Then along came the Sunday Schools, giving much needed tuition to the masses. This was dangerous; it fuelled civil disobedience or so the authorities believed. The fact that the Methodists were spurred by no such motives was irrelevant. In Nottingham alone some 1,700 children were, by 1802, receiving a regular dose of reading, writing and summing.

The New Connexion at Hucknall were hated. Their properties were vandalised and attempts made to burn down their places of learning and worship. Undeterred, in 1808, they opened the very Sunday School which the then infant Elizabeth Sheppard began to attend.

In the nearby village of Calverton in 1790, a meeting house run by the Methodist minister John Roe was opened where he defied the establishment by openly conducting marriage ceremonies of his own formulation. Quite how, if at all, they differed from the accepted ceremony I have no idea, but they certainly offended the protectors of mainstream religion and possibly offered women a status somewhat above that of chattel, to the extent that complaints resulted in the arrest and imprisonment of several women of Roe's flock for the taking of heretic vows. Their actual crime was described as *refusal to swear to the fathers of their children.* They quite rightly protested that they were as married as anyone else, but to no avail. Their pleas went unheard and they were given substantial prison sentences. Interestingly, I never came across any records to indicate the punishment of any men for similar crimes.

***

I don't recall exactly when it was that I located Bess' home. Being blind to the fact that what had begun as mere idle curiosity was expanding exponentially into full blown obsession and not realising that what might make for idle chit-chat were I ever to find myself in the unlikely setting of a cocktail party was to one day aspire to book form, I neglected the keeping of comprehensive records. Consequently, when I come to look for the date I first found her house, it's missing.

The exact location was something that nagged at me. From the dissenter's letter in the Review I knew she lived a mile or thereabouts from the church. The report of the murder in the same organ, I knew, described it as being beside Robinson's Mill. But who was this Robinson? There was little else to go on.

35

From the layout of Papplewick I knew that the Sheppard family couldn't have lived to the north of the village for the church itself was almost at the northern limit and beyond there was but Papplewick Hall, the sumptuous home of the Whig MP Frederick Montagu, and Newstead Park itself. Perhaps the house had been demolished. That, however, seemed unlikely for there were within the precincts of the village many cottages of sturdy stone construction, clearly dated upon their stone lintels with inscriptions from before Bess' time. I assumed that the house she had lived in would be of similarly sturdy construction and would have survived.

I turned my attention to the south. A drive of less than half a mile from the church brought me to the Griffin's Head cross road. Resisting valiantly the temptation to drop in the pub I concluded that to make up the balance of the mile or more they were said to have lived from the church, I had three options. If, as was said, they lived near the mill, then east was out for it led away from the River Leen, the only possible site for a mill. A right turn at the cross road took me due west toward Papplewick's twin, with which it shared Thomas Hurt as vicar, the picturesque village of Linby. Straight across, due south, followed the course of the river. I turned west.

Within a couple of hundred yards is a lay-by with a picnic site attached from which one can gain access to the river. In the lay-by a sign detailed the route of a leisurely walk around the flood dykes on the river. What was more important though, it showed the location of Robinson's mills. Plural.

One of the mills, it seemed, had stood just across the road from where I was parked. Bearing in mind the letter had specified that the mill was a mile from the churchyard I might not have bothered, but fired up with finding the name Robinson I crossed over to what I found out later was Castle Mill. It had been converted by some enterprising

36

entrepreneur into flats for those wealthy enough to afford such prestigious properties. Somehow neglecting to notice the distinct scarcity of lesser status dwellings in the immediate locale I knocked on the heavy oak door. A lady answered the door and was courteous enough not to immediately slam it. I asked her somewhat naively if she knew anything of the history of the building. She replied, unsurprisingly, that she did. Money buys not just property, but history too - and preferably a tortured one.

The occupant claimed it was one of Robinson's Mills and took me out to see the old mill race by the side of the building. The site of another mill, she told me, was supposedly somewhere further down the river. Her husband was a local radio DJ and later trips past the place revealed him to be the owner of a beautiful Rolls Royce. Sadly, I never had to return there. Bess' home was elsewhere.

It lay to the south of the village. No sooner had I driven down from the Griffin I realised it was the most likely location. The village stretched in this direction much further than any other and with an abundance of houses that might fit the bill. Part way down I turned right onto the Hucknall road. A row of cottages beside the river had been converted into one dwelling by its current owner. It bore the name Warp Mill. I walked up the gravel drive and knocked on the door. I explained to the man who answered what I was doing; he was a superior kind of fellow judging from the bags in the knees of his expensive corduroys. If there was a history attached to this place, he'd know. I mentioned Bess. He stared back at me, scratched his bald head and looked blank. As I was leaving his driveway, taking care to disturb the gravel as little as possible, he called after me.

"You should try Bill," he said. "Don't know his second name but he lives down there somewhere on the opposite side, He's in his nineties, but if anyone knows anything, Bill will."

I waved my thanks and went in search of Bill. It would be good to say I found him and he was the answer to all my prayers, but I didn't so he wasn't. It was getting late in the evening and I was hungry. Dusk was clinging damply to me. I looked for the kind of place that might be the stereotypical home of a nonagenarian. Net curtains, aspidistras, dusty ornaments on window ledges or chrysanthemums in gardens with paper bags on their heads to capture earwigs; anything.

Nothing. I made a detour down a farm lane to turn my car round. The farmer was making last minute adjustments to his tractor ready for the morning and eyed me suspiciously as I braked. Though he didn't say what's a stranger like you doing in these parts, he easily could have. He was, it transpired, very friendly. Parrot-like I explained my business. Bess. Robinson. The lot. He pushed back a fawn denim cap from his dusty forehead and, raising his arm, pointed to a honey coloured ruin just behind me to the left.

"That," he explained," used to be the Grange where old Robinson used to live. See that wall where the cars are parked? That's the only bit left." He indicated the scant remains of a wall on my immediate left.

"Them's Robinson's stables," he continued.

"The cottages I'm after were next to the mill," I said. He swung his arm round and pointed at nothing.

"That were the mill," he said, and I noticed what was now no more than a dip in the green field in which a dozen Friesians lazily grazed. "Beyond were the millpond."

"And were there any cottages with the mill?" I asked.

"Back there a touch," he said. "D'you see that row standing back beyond the Green?" I nodded. "That were Grange Cottages. Robinson's cottages."

38

I looked back to where he was pointing and saw the row standing back from, and parallel to, the road. A second small group stood at right angles to them to their rear.

"You've heard of Bess?" I asked.

"Course," he nodded.

"Do you know that's where she lived?"

"Had to have been," he replied.

I thanked him and left. It was too late to approach the cottages that evening though I desperately wanted to talk to the residents. Had anything been passed down over the years? Any local knowledge? A number had been roughly boarded up, but there were quite enough still occupied to make a return visit essential.

***

Robinson was a very rich man. He was also, I concluded fairly quickly, a bastard. Of Scottish descent, he owned six mills on the Leen between Papplewick and Bulwell, then a neighbouring village a few miles hence. The more generous of his contemporaries described him as *a man possessed of great business talent, energy and capital.* There was no mention of compassion.

He lived in Papplewick Grange, a manor house at the southernmost edge of the village, and was the proud owner of many a fancy gig and thoroughbred horse, dressing always in tailored clothes and moving in the fanciest of circles. He accumulated wealth as a mill owner from the manufacture of broad loom fabric at his various sites. Vast fortunes could be made from the supplying of cloth to be made into uniforms for the soldiers fighting Napoleon. Such contracts were highly lucrative, through the exploitation of the working classes they exacted a high price. Such exploitation was commonplace and in early 19th Century

England it was routine to include within those available, the children. Robinson, keen to remain a success and ahead of the pack, would sustain the lifestyle to which he had become accustomed by shipping in youngsters, mainly orphans and street urchins, from the slums of London. Kids without family to care for them. Kids who, from Robinson's perspective, had no future anyway and were, consequently, no loss. He set them to work in his mills in conditions of appalling deprivation. Their hard lives were thankfully short. An official survey was carried out in 1816. This is part of its report:

The facts we collected seemed to me to be terrible almost beyond belief. Not in exceptional cases but as a rule, we found children of 10 regularly worked 14 hours a day, but with half an hour's interval for the midday meal, which was eaten in the factory. In the fine yarn cotton mills they were subjected to this labour in a temperature usually exceeding 75 degrees; and in all the cotton factories they breathed in atmospheres more or less injurious to their lungs, because of the dust and minute cotton fibres that pervaded it. In some cases we found that greed of gain had impelled the mill owners to still greater extremes of inhumanity, utterly disgraceful indeed to a civilised nation. The mills were run 15 and in some cases 16 hours a day with a single set of hands, and they did not scruple to employ children of both sexes from the age of 8. We actually found a number below that age.

This report, remember, was written in 1816, at the time when England was not a liberal country. In that same year Robert Peel pronounced that, come the end of the war, the minimum age for employing children in factories should be, not increased, but *reduced* to 9 and the hours, not decreased, but *increased* to 13 from the far too lenient 12. Not everyone held Peel's opinion. A parliamentary petition at the time stated:

....depriving parents of sufficient employ makes them dependent on their children for support; which as experience too tragically proves, deprives them of the authority over youth which is necessary to retard the progress of vice and promote virtue. The evils of factory life are incalculable.....

The children of Papplewick and Linby suffered greatly. Many of the infants employed by Robinson died in harness. The Linby and Papplewick Notebook kept by Reverend Illingworth Butler records no fewer than 163 children were buried at one time in a mass, unmarked grave in Linby churchyard, all victims of the mills. The parish register details just 42 such children. To argue that the discrepancy is due to inaccurately maintained records or under-recording to minimise the tragedies is to miss the point. Whatever the numbers involved, the culpability of Robinson and his kind is established.

Not only did Robinson cause the deaths of local and imported children alike, he also, by virtue of his policy of employing the vulnerable young, deprived the men of the area, the handloom knitters, of their livelihood. He inevitably attracted the attention of the Luddites.

On November 4th 1811, upwards of one thousand men gathered at the Seven Mile House (the ginger beer house at which Rotherham was later to call) and, armed with anything they could use as a weapon, planned to march on Sutton-in-Ashfield, smashing mill frames en route. Robinson could not escape this onslaught. He would have been a prime target. Hopelessly outnumbered, the constable could do nothing. Robinson must have been a frightened man. In 1812 he issued a bizarre handbill offering a reward to those who would collaborate in smashing the Luddites. It read:

£100 REWARD - THREATENING LETTER

WHEREAS A PARCEL DIRECTED TO MR GASCON

OF HUCKNALL, WAS FOUND NEAR THE DWELLING HOUSE

OF THE REVEREND LUKE JACKSON AT HUCKNALL TORKARD

CONTAINING A LETTER, WHICH MR JACKSON DELIVERED

TO HIS NEIGHBOUR MR J ROBINSON, PAPPLEWICK,

YESTERDAY, AND OF WHICH THIS IS A COPY:

MR ROBINSON, IF YOU DO NOT TURN MR SAVEL AWAY YOUR

MILL WILL BE BURNT DOWN BY FIRE FOR GETTING ME MEN TANE.

GENERAL LUDD.

IF YOU PROSECUTE ANY OF MY MEN NEDI SHALL VISIT YOU GENTLEMEN - PERSECUTE ANY OF MY MEN IF YOU DURST.

THERE BE MANY OF YOU GENTLEMEN TO HIE BY YOUR HEADS.

GEN. LUDD.

I'VE GUNS AND POWDER AND BALL. PAPPLEWICK.

The General Ludd to whom the letter referred was the supposed eponymous leader of the Luddites, Ned Ludd. Whether he truly existed is doubtful, but his name was adopted by both rebels and authorities alike. He struck fear into the hearts of mill owners. The authorities, being unable to catch him, portrayed him as a phantom, materialising in

42

countless disguises and capable of vanishing like a wisp of smoke.

The leases on Robinson's mills finally expired in 1840. Andrew Montagu, the son of Frederick and now lord of Papplewick Hall, closed the mills and demolished the forty-four foot mill wheels. The centre for cotton production moved to Lancashire and Robinson's empire came to an end.

Satisfying though it would be, I cannot inform you that this was an end to Robinson's good fortune. He transferred his wealth to Nottingham and, with that *great business talent, energy and capital,* opened up yet another lucrative operation. It will come as no surprise to find that this pariah entered the world of banking, founding, from the proceeds of countless children's deaths, the Moore and Robinson Bank. Papplewick Grange was demolished in 1846. An era of great evil was over.

Records show that one child at least survived the hell of the mill. One John Axford came up from the London slums in the 1790s and stayed on to marry a local girl, another Elizabeth. In 1817, when Bess went to Mansfield on that fateful day, she took with her an umbrella. The umbrella belonged to Elizabeth Axford. Elizabeth Axford was subsequently a witness at the trial of Charles Rotherham.

***

I pulled my car in across the road from where the farmer had said Bess had lived and sat staring for some time at the stone cottage. Its solid, clean construction clashed with the mental image of a shambling but idyllic home I had imagined for them - all creaking timbers and lupins by the gate. This was not the romanticised residence of fictional peasants of yore, it was a functional, labourer's home.

43

In front of the row of cottages stretched a wide expanse of overgrown grass that reached from the doorways fifty or sixty feet to the road. Had Bess once played right here? Had this piece of ground once been cultivated to feed the family? There were times when I almost felt I could conjure up in the present a physical reality from the past. It was an uncomfortable feeling. I felt I was intruding. It was as if, were I to persevere long enough, I would be rewarded with some glimpse into the past. I need scarcely say, I was not.

As I had anticipated, the lure of the cottages gave reward more to the overworked imagination than to reality. A number were unoccupied, some were boarded up and held back from the market by a property developer expecting to one day make a killing. Ironically, if my story ever made it into print, it might only serve to push up his asking price. One old lady spoke with me at length but was unable to tell me anything that added to my knowledge. She did, however, let me have a quick look round at the small, cramped rooms. Though one of these terraced cottages was Bess' home, I derived no sense of her from them. I left, grateful to the old lady, but a little disappointed.

***

The more steeped I became in Bess' time, the closer I felt myself growing to her. I would run through the story in my head last thing at night only to find it, for a long time, the first thing on my mind the following morning. I was being taken over by her. She exerted a considerable influence over me down the years, so much so that I did begin to feel the bloody events of 1817 and the mystery of the twenty-four hours surrounding her death demanded a real, physical need for the full story to be unearthed and told. The disquiet I experienced in the vicinity of the stone was at times so intense that the only way I could imagine dispelling it was to re-tell the tale. The trouble was, I was becoming unsure

44

just who exactly was making these demands of me. I had imagined at the start that it had been, if anyone, Bess. Now I wasn't sure. Maybe Charles Rotherham, too, wanted the story told. Could it be they were both reaching for me? Were they both demanding my attention? Maybe there was something to this paranormal nonsense. But then, maybe I was just going nuts.

I could not deny that both the location of the murder *and* the site of Bess' grave seemed permeated by an intensity whose origin was unknown. Bess and Rotherham belonged to no-one. It was achingly sad. Many is the time I stood either by the stone on the road or in the graveyard and talked to Bess as if she was there, asking for just a clue as to what happened that day in July so long ago.

It was a comfort to discover I was not the sole victim of the seductive power of the story. The stone, over the years, had become the target of graffiti artists who had chiselled into its soft surface. It was last renovated in 1910 but further damage had since been done. A stone orb that had once topped the monument had long since been lost. Then, in the 1980s, Richard Morley came on the scene.

Richard was a factory worker from Sutton-in-Ashfield and in his early twenties. How his actions can be attributed to anything but the pull of the girl I have no idea. He, too, is at a loss to explain it. His first sight of the stone so gripped him that, there and then, he resolved to give up his job, become a stone mason and restore it. And that's what he did. Richard found work with the masons responsible for nearby Hardwick Hall, once home of Bess of Hardwick. There he learned his trade and honed his skills, devoting his spare time to the long, arduous task of re-furbishing the stone, removing the damage of seventy odd years from its face. To do this, because the inscriptions were so low down and moving the stone was out of the question, he dug trenches around the base in which he would stand in order to work on

45

the stone at eye level. Meticulously he ground away at its surface, millimetre by painstaking millimetre, until it was ready to receive its newly carved inscription.

Richard Morley is a caring person. His renovation of the stone was completed on the whim of no local dignitary, nor did he, for his efforts, receive any payment. He is not, as far as either of us are aware, related in any way to the Sheppard family. It was, simply - and inexplicably - an act of personal generosity. He would, perhaps, deny it now, but the change he allowed Bess to make to his life was utterly illogical. He was, it seems, like me, taken over by something neither of us can explain to this day.

***

I returned to the press of 1817 where the story was still unfolding. In the Nottingham Review of August 1st I found this report of Charles Rotherham's trial:

Charles Rotherham, aged 33, was arraigned on a charge of wilfully murdering Elizabeth Sheppard on the 7th of July. To this charge he pleaded guilty, but at the earnest solicitation of the learned judge he was prevailed upon to retract his plea.

Sergeant Vaughan conducted the prosecution, and called upon Mary Sheppard, the unhappy mother of the unfortunate girl, who appeared in the box clothed in black, and the picture of distress. This poor woman told the court that her daughter would have been seventeen years of age had she lived a few days longer. She left her mother's house between twelve and one on the 7th of July for the purpose of going to Mansfield to seek work. She described the dress, and said she had on a pair of shoes which were new the Sunday before, and had with her a light coloured umbrella. Witness went out about a quarter to six, and walked as far as the toll bar in expectation of meeting her, but saw

46

nothing of her and turned back; never saw her again until about a quarter of an hour before she was taken out of the house to be buried. Is sure it was her daughter.

Sarah Clay lives in Mansfield in the employ of Messrs. Hancock and Wakefield. She saw Elizabeth Sheppard at Mansfield about half past four o'clock in the afternoon of the 7th of July. Elizabeth left Mansfield on her return to Papplewick about three minutes before six. She saw her again on the roadside, about three miles from Mansfield, but she was dead, and some men were putting her in a cart to convey her to Sutton.

William Thompson lives in Mansfield, he had been to Nottingham on the 7th of July and was on his return home. Between six and seven he met the prisoner about a mile from the spot where the murder was done, between the second and third milestone from Mansfield; is sure the prisoner is the man. He saw a young woman on the same side of the road, she was then following him, at a distance of two or three hundred yards; the prisoner had nothing in his hands. She was a young woman about seventeen years of age and he saw the body afterward, it was the same person. He saw nobody else on the road.

Thomas Highgate had been to Red Hill on the 7th of July, to a commissioner's meeting. Red Hill is about nine and a half miles from Mansfield. About seven o'clock he met the prisoner at the bar about halfway between the toll bar and the Rainworth Water, being perhaps a third of a mile from the place where the body was found afterwards. He had then a bundle in his left hand and an umbrella in his right.

William Ball is a soldier of the 9th Regiment on foot, and on the evening of the 7th of July was on the road between Nottingham and Mansfield. He met the prisoner at the bar about one hundred yards on the Nottingham side of the Hutt, about three quarters of a mile from the spot where the

47

body afterward was found, and Rotherham offered him a pint of beer if he would turn back to the public house with him. Witness accepted the offer, and when they were there, prisoner told him that his wife had run away, and taken all his clothes with her. Witness remained in the house about a quarter of an hour.

Robert Cheadle was at the Three Crowns public house in Red Hill, about half past nine o'clock in the evening of the 7th of July; while he was there a man came in who called himself Charles Rotherham, and they had some conversation together. The prisoner at the bar is the man; he called for a cup of ale, and complained of being much tired, for he had come thirty-six miles that day; he had a pair of shoes and an umbrella in his hand; he said his wife had gone away with all his clothes, he had but two shillings in his pocket, and offered to sell the shoes for two shillings, stating they were his wife's shoes.

Mary Pettinger lives at the Three Crowns, Red Hill, and remembers the prisoner coming to her house on the 7th of July; he had a pair of shoes, a small bundle, and an umbrella with him; he slept there at night, and left the house about seven the next morning, after he was gone, the shoes he brought with him were found at the foot of the bed, she took them downstairs and delivered one to Barnes, the constable; Robert Whitworth fetched the other.

John Womley lives at Mansfield; about a quarter past six in the morning he went to work; when he got fifty or sixty yards beyond the third milestone he found a button and soon after a ball of cloth. About half past nine he discovered the body of a young woman, lying in the ditch, about seven yards from the place where he had found the things, he did not take the body out of the ditch immediately, but sent to inform Colonel Need and lawyer Walkden; about two o'clock he took the body from the ditch, and found the skull broken on one side; he could not describe her wounds, her

48

head was so disfigured, a large hedgestake lay by the body about a foot and a half from her head; her petticoat lay at her feet and her shawl upon her bonnet above her head, the hedgestake was all over blood; he put her in the cart, for conveyance to Sutton.

Richard Jepson, the constable of Sutton, was sent for on the morning of the 8th, and picked up the stake by the side of the body. The witness produced the stake in court; it was between four and five feet long and still bore evident marks of blood upon it, and its appearance evidently struck feelings of horror into the court.

John Batchelor, a surgeon of Sutton, was called upon to view the body while it lay in the ditch, the head was completely covered with blood, there was an extensive fracture on one side of the skull, which was broken in on the brain, and another fracture on the left side; the wounds were inflicted by some blunt instrument and were very likely to have been done by the hedgestake; had no doubt that the wounds were the cause of the young woman's death.

Ann Lewis keeps a public house in Bunny; on the morning of the 8th of July, the prisoner at the bar called there, and had an umbrella with him, he offered it for sale, and she bought it; witness afterwards gave it to constable Barnes.

Benjamin Barnes is a constable and was sent in search of the prisoner, about half past one o'clock in the afternoon of the 8th of July; he heard of him at Bunny, and first saw him about half a mile from Loughborough, where he apprehended him, he saw spots of blood on his coat collar and neck handkerchief, first took him to Bunny, to Lewis where he found the umbrella, the prisoner denied all knowledge at first but afterward he acknowledged it. He brought him to Nottingham, and lodged him in the county gaol. On Wednesday witness took him to Sutton-in-Ashfield, where the coroner's court was sitting; no threats or promises had been held out to him to induce him to confess, many persons crowded into the room where he was in custody; in order to see him, and to this witness objected, but the prisoner said,

"Never mind, let them come forward, I am guilty of the crime, and must take the course of the law."

As they were returning to Nottingham, they passed that part of the road where the body was found, and, when near the spot, the prisoner said, (pointing to a part of the hedge),

"That is the place where I drew out the hedgestake."

This was on the contrary side of the road to where the murder was committed, the prisoner observed that he could not tell what possessed him at that moment, he never spoke to the woman, but the moment he got up to her, he struck her on the head and repeated the blows until she was lifeless; the prisoner said he had turned out her pockets inside out, but there was nothing in them, and he did undo her stays at the front, in expectation of finding something concealed, but found nothing, all he had taken from her was the pair of shoes and the umbrella. He told witnesses he had left the shoes at the Three Crowns, in the room in which he slept and further said he had six shillings in his pocket at the time he committed the murder. Witness produced one shoe which he received from Mr Lewis.

Joseph Barrows looked at the shoe, he made it for her, the deceased, and delivered it to her hand.

Elizabeth Axford lent Elizabeth Sheppard the umbrella, just before she set out for Mansfield, and identified it as her property.

The jury returned a verdict of guilty, and his lordship immediately passed the awful sentence of the law upon him, *namely, that he should be hanged on Monday, and his body given to the surgeons for dissection.*

Fourteen witnesses in all were called, each in turn giving evidence that filled in the last twenty-four hours of Bessie Sheppard's life from her leaving home on the 7th of July to her being dragged dead from the ditch on the afternoon of the 8th. She was identified as the girl seen on the road by witnesses who later saw her body in death. Seven witnesses gave evidence of contact with Rotherham himself, all were able to identify him as the man they had seen on the 7th or the 8th. It seemed so conclusive. The weight of evidence was overwhelming. Rotherham had even confessed his guilt to Benjamin Barnes, the constable. There seemed to be little more to be said. Rotherham was guilty and deserved his fate.

I didn't sleep that night. The names of witnesses and their testimony swirled round in my head. It just didn't *feel* right, though what the exact nature of the worry was I had no idea. Rotherham had pleaded guilty for heaven's sake. It was only at the insistence of the judge that he changed his plea to not guilty. Despite the judge's efforts to be fair, the evidence had been damning. Rotherham had been found guilty and sentenced to hang. Leaving aside my inherent hatred of the death penalty, quite what was my problem? I was married to my first wife at that time. She got little sleep that night. I ran and re-ran the evidence past her continually. It was not until late into the night that, more out of exasperation and exhaustion rather than concern for Rotherham, she said,

"What's the problem? Don't you think he did it?"

I found myself shaking my head.

"No," I replied, "I don't."

But I hadn't the slightest idea why.

51

***

One further visit to Angel Row was sufficient to provide me with what I believed was the full story, at least as far as contemporaneous news accounts were concerned. In the August 2nd edition of the Nottingham Journal was this account of the trial and execution of Charles Rotherham:

The only capital cases were those of George Bates and Joseph Lees.....and Charles Rotherham, for the wilful murder of Elizabeth Sheppard on the 7th of July inst., in the parish of Sutton-in-Ashfield. The latter case provides a striking instance of the speedy vengeance which following the perpetration of the crime, not quite three weeks having elapsed from the time when the murder was committed, to the period when the criminal expiated his offences on the public gallows! It is also to be observed that the crime was marked with this peculiar feature, that the prisoner had received no provocation, nor could he assign any other motive for his inhuman conduct, than a sudden and fell desire, which took possession of his mind, to destroy the girl! According to his own testimony he had set out from Sheffield for the purpose of seeking employment as a haymaker, and on his way toward Nottingham he overtook the unhappy object of his sanguinary ferocity; he passed her without taking any particular notice, and proceeded on, till feeling himself weary, he sat down by the road to rest. Just as the woman came up, the horrid idea entered his mind of murdering her, he instantly seized a stake out of the hedge and going up softly behind her, without speaking one word, he struck her a violent blow on the head. She cried, "Oh Dear" and fell, when he repeated his blows till she was dead. He then left her in the dreadful state in which she was found (about fifty yards past the third milestone on the road from Mansfield) and pursued his journey, without ever reflecting on what he had done. On Friday afternoon the prisoner (Charles Rotherham) was arraigned at the bar of

52

Justice, charged on the Coroner's inquest with the wilful murder of Elizabeth Sheppard. He pleaded guilty to the indictment proffered against him; but at the suggestion of the learned judge, he withdrew his plea, and the trial was proceeded with.

Mary Sheppard, mother of the deceased, gave evidence as to the girl leaving her home at Papplewick between twelve and one o'clock on Monday the 7th of July to go to Mansfield, for the purposes of seeking work; that she was nearly 17 years old, and had an umbrella with her and a pair of shoes which she had bought new the Sunday before. Other witnesses were brought forward to show that she was seen between three and four miles from Mansfield on her way home, about seven o'clock, that the prisoner (Rotherham) was at that time a few yards from her, and that on the morning about half past nine o'clock, her mangled remains were discovered by a man of the name Womley, lying in a ditch, a short distance from the third milestone. Her head presented a most frightful appearance being covered with blood, and the skull beaten in on both sides. Her bonnet and shawl lay at a distance, and about a foot and a half from the body, a large hedgestake lay, with marks of blood upon it. (The hedgestake was produced, and excited feelings of horror throughout the whole court.)

The prisoner was next seen at the Hutt, where he had two pints of ale with an acquaintance whom he accidentally met; from thence he was traced to the Ginger Beer House where he had two glasses of peppermint; and the next place he was seen was the Three Crowns, Red Hill about half past nine in the evening. Here he took up his abode for the night and offered a pair of women's shoes for sale, which afterward proved to be the same worn by the deceased, but meeting with no purchaser, he left them in the bedroom. On the next day (Tuesday July 8th) the prisoner travelled to Nottingham and after stopping about an hour and a half went on to

53

Bunny, where he sold the umbrella, taken from the girl, to Mrs Lewis. From thence he proceeded towards Loughborough and was finally taken by Barnes and Linneker, two Nottingham police officers, whilst looking over a bridge near Loughborough. He was brought to Nottingham and lodged in the county gaol the same evening, and the next day (Wednesday) was conveyed to Sutton-in-Ashfield, for examination before the Coroner's Jury, upon whose verdict he was committed by the Coroner for trial. Whilst under examination at Sutton, many persons pressed to get sight of him, which Barnes, who had him in charge, objected to, but the prisoner desired that they might be allowed to come forward, as he was guilty of the crime imputed to him, and must take the course of the law.

Barnes related a conversation which took place between him and the prisoner on their way back to the county gaol, from which it appeared, that when they arrived near the spot where the murdered body was found, Rotherham pointed to a hedge on the opposite side of the road and said :- That was the place where he drew out the stake with which he killed the young woman. He did not know what possessed him, neither party had spoken to each other, but as soon as he got up to her, he struck her on the head and followed up his blows until he killed her. He then turned her pockets inside out, but found nothing; he also unlaced her stays at the front, in the expectation of finding something concealed, but in this was likewise disappointed, and he took nothing from her but her umbrella and shoes. He could not tell what it was that urged him to the deed, as he had sixpence in his pocket at the time.

The prisoner when called upon for his defence was silent, and the Jury without hesitation pronounced him guilty.

The learned judge then proceeded to pass sentence of death upon him, in the most awful and impressive terms, which he heard with much fortitude than might have been expected from one in his dreadful plight. He stood perfectly collected during the whole trial, and seemed to have reconciled himself to the dreadful fate which awaited him. Both before and after condemnation, the wretched culprit listened with earnest attention to the pious exhortations of the Reverend the Chaplain, and Mr Bryan, a dissenting Minister, who attended him in his devotions to the last moment. During his confinement he has invariably disavowed making any attack upon the girl's chastity, as no such designs ever entered his mind, neither had he any intention at the time of robbing her.

On Sunday the Reverend Dr Wood delivered an impressive discourse to the unfortunate man, whose feelings seemed much affected, as his eyes were frequently suffused with tears, and he seemed in evident concern respecting the state of his soul.

Before seven o'clock on Monday morning the unhappy criminal was led forth, and being placed in a cart, was conveyed to the usual place of execution on Gallow's Hill, where he resigned himself to his ignominious fate in a frame of mind which indicated repentance, but gave no assurances of happiness hereafter. The culprit was hanged with his irons on and struggled a great deal. Not less than 18 or 20,000 people attended the execution. His body hanging the usual time, was given to the surgeons for dissection, and after such operations were performed upon it as were deemed necessary it was publically exposed on Tuesday in the County Hall, previous to its being interred in St Mary's churchyard.

Rotherham was about 33 or 34 years of age, with an overhanging brow and a malignant cast of features. He was a native of Sheffield, where he had a wife but no children, and one brother and two sisters now living. He had served for upward of twelve years as a soldier in the corps of the Artillery Drivers, had been present in many battles in Egypt,

55

Portugal, Spain and France, and obtained his discharge at the conclusion of the Peace, in 1815. On the day of the murder he said he had drunk seven pints of ale in Mansfield.

The Nottingham Review said of the execution:

Execution of Charles Rotherham, - On Monday morning soon after six o'clock, the body of this unhappy criminal was demanded by the Sheriff at the county gaol. On this occasion the execution did not take place before the prison, but at the usual place, on the forest, known by the name of Gallow's Hill. He was placed in a cart, and attended by the Reverend J Bryan, the minister of the Zion chapel, who has unremittingly visited him in the prison, ever since the 17th of July. Mr George Baxter of Bingham was also in the cart. The mournful cavalcade proceeded through the town, attended by a less number of spectators than usual, but by the time it arrived at the fatal tree, the concourse of people was immense, it is supposed much larger than was ever collected in that place on a similar occasion. The Reverend J Bryan addressed the multitude at great length, particularly pointing out the evil consequences of drunkenness. Rotherham did not speak at all, but after a few minutes spent in prayer the cart was drawn away and he was launched into eternity. His body was taken to the County Hall, and on Tuesday, after the surgeons had performed their duty, he was exposed to public view in the Nisi Prius Court. In the evening his remains were interred at the back of St Mary's church. He was born in Sheffield in the year 1784, his parents are both dead, but he has left a wife, one brother and two sisters, to lament his untimely fate. He was at a proper age put apprentice to a Mr Parker, scissor grinder, of Sheffield with whom he served his time, except the last year, which he bought out; he soon after enlisted as a driver in the Artillery, in which he continued twelve years and twenty-one days, when he was discharged by roll. During his time he was in many engagements and sieges without ever receiving a wound, viz., in Egypt, Flushing, Maida, Ciudad Rodrigo, Badajoz, Salamanca, Toulouse, etc., etc.,.

If that was the full story, and I had no reason to doubt it, it did nothing to alleviate the fact that the evidence seemed damning. Charles Rotherham was, it appeared, guilty and, insofar as anyone deserved such a fate, he deserved to hang.

My own views on capital punishment had been fixed for years. I have never been able to accept that any act of violence, no matter how horrific, could ever justify the state reciprocating and taking another life. The contrived death of an individual at the hands of the state, to my mind, serves only to demean the species of which I am a part. Vengeance may occupy some understandable place in the human heart, but it has none in the statutes of any society that claims for itself the term *civilised*.

Often promulgated is the notion of deterrence. Whatever its validity today, if we try to assess its effect in 1817, we must first consider just what crime it was that the state wanted to deter the felon from committing. The nature of both what constitutes a crime and with what severity that crime should be dealt has varied throughout history, dependent upon prevailing attitudes and the overall moral climate of the nation. In 1817 Britain was emerging from - and shortly due to re-enter - a time of extreme turbulence. Riots caused by food shortages and growing unemployment, the disruptive activities of the Luddites, the suffocating effect upon the economy of the return from the war with Napoleon of many thousands of ex-soldiers, the instability of the monarchy of George III, the recent revolution in France, the loss of the Americas - all these things conspired to create in Britain a repressive and punitive legislature whose sole aim was to stifle any inclination to armed rebellion by the masses.

There were, accordingly, upward of two hundred offences listed on the statute that attracted the death penalty. Regency England, however, was reluctant to carry it out. Indeed, this reluctance in 1817 resulted in, out of the several hundred potentially capital offences being brought before the Nottingham Assizes, just two hangings. Charles Rotherham was one. For the ordinary citizen to have been influenced in his actions by the deterrent effect of the gallows, it would have been necessary to possess an encyclopaedic knowledge of the judicial system.

There were some notable - and amusing - judgements. On July 14th a youth was convicted of 'seducing a lady'. He was sentenced at his trial in Nottingham to drink two pints of onion broth and then be hanged by his feet for twenty minutes, after which ordeal he was required to consume a further two pints of the obnoxious brew.

In the same July the Pentrich riots took place. Three hundred men led by one Jeremiah Brandreth of Sutton-in-Ashfield marched on Nottingham protesting against high food prices and low wages. Within the protester's midst was a government *agent provocateur* known as Oliver the Spy. Acting on orders, Oliver incited the men to acts of violence which they would otherwise likely not have committed but for his encouragement. Brandreth and forty-one of his co-conspirators were brought before the same Grand Jury as Rotherham, charged with treason or, as the records state, with being:

"...seduced by the instigation of the Devil as false traitors against our Lord, the King."

Brandreth and co. were eventually tried in Derby in the October of that year. The majority were sentenced to deportation to the colonies. Special treatment was reserved for the ringleaders.

"You, and each of you, shall be taken from hence to the gaol from whence you came and thence be drawn on a hurdle to the place of execution and there be severally hanged by the neck until you are dead - and thereafterward your heads shall be severed from your bodies and your bodies, divided into four quarters, shall be disposed of as his Majesty shall direct, and may the Lord God of all Mercies have compassion upon you."

By 1817 George III had no real power. Though in his younger days an effective and relatively compassionate monarch, by 1817 he was suffering from the disease porphyria, which mimicked insanity. With purple urine and a sensitivity to light that caused his skin to blister, coupled with the tendency to manic raving, he was declared insane. The Regent - after whom the times are named, the Prince of Wales and subsequent George IV - assumed effective control. Acting nominally on behalf of the King (by now into the last three years of his life) he exercised his compassion on Brandreth and his men. His clemency didn't however extend to commuting their sentences to deportation. No, Brandreth and his comrades were kept, by the Regent's profound magnanimity, from the indignity of being ritually quartered. They were, however, still hanged.

History it seems has forgiven them. A street in the modern Sutton-in-Ashfield is named after Jeremiah Brandreth.

***

What had begun as such a sketchy story - indeed, a postscript even in local history - was now gathering momentum and expanding at such a rate I was becoming, at times, swamped by information. There still remained yawning gaps in my knowledge that I feared would never be filled. What was Rotherham like as a man? He'd fought for his country, certainly, something which today may have caused him to be held in greater esteem than he experienced. Was there anything I could learn of him, or was he destined to remain a mere cipher for hatred? Were there any clues in his testimony? Why, for example, had the judge insisted he change his plea from guilty to not guilty? Was it a simple act in the pursuance of justice?

But, at his trial, Rotherham said nothing. Not one word in either defence or mitigation. There were, however, many references to his alleged confessions. Why was it that a man with apparently so profligate a tendency to confess was denied the ideal platform upon which he could give his greatest performance? The Nottingham Journal of August 2nd is incorrect when it states,

"...according to his own testimony he had set out from Sheffield...,"

Charles Rotherham never testified. Indeed, later in their own account they write,

"The prisoner when called upon for his defence was silent..."

If they had these alleged confessions and they knew Rotherham had only withdrawn his guilty plea on the insistence of the judge, why go to the trouble of so comprehensive an airing of the evidence? Could it have been that the authorities wanted to stage some piece of macabre theatre for the public? Did they seek to make an example of Charles Rotherham?

Brandreth and Co., whose activities threatened the fabric of law and order, were in the same gaol at the same time as Rotherham. They were due to appear the next day. What an opportunity for the judge to use Rotherham - a man clearly heading for the gallows - to demonstrate to those members of the public the folly of seeking any solution to their misery through disobedience.

He may well be guilty and yet, here I was, developing a burgeoning sympathy for the man. There was, or so it seemed to me, a great sadness surrounding him. He may not have been a good man, but that did not mean he was no good. There have been enough cases over the years where judicial certainty has been later exposed to be, at best, police exuberance, and at worst, downright corruption. None among us is able to say, hand on heart, that the verdict of the courts invariably reflects the truth. All too frequently this has been found not to be the case, and, all too frequently it was never even *intended* to be the case. In more celebrated cases the verdict is eventually challenged. In Charles Rotherham's case, it was not. No-one ever spoke up for him.

I knew that I was coming to the conclusion, somewhat reluctantly, that if anyone was to speak on his behalf, it would have to be me. Volunteers were hardly beating down the door. It was Bess to whom I'd originally been drawn and to contemplate anything but outright condemnation of Rotherham felt a little like betrayal. Was my allegiance to Bess so fragile that, on a whim, I could realign my sympathies with her likely killer?

For a while I didn't visit the grave. I would return there one day if, and only if, I could satisfy myself that it transpired there was substance to Rotherham's defence. One thing remained clear. A great injustice had been done. The needless slaying of Elizabeth Sheppard. But was it possible it was she *and* Rotherham calling to me down the ages? Could it be they were trying to tell me not just of the injustice to Bess, but also of similar perpetrated on Rotherham?

Everyone in the saga was dead. Could it be that some alternative truth, were it to be discovered, would have a momentum of its own? What skeletons, left in peace all this time, was it possible to disturb?

Bess was taking over my life. This crusade, if you will, was totally within my own mind. Nobody else gave a damn. It would have been so convenient to just block it out, but I couldn't. If no-one else cared, did that make my caring wrong? History had transformed itself, quite spectacularly, from the empty contemplation of things of little consequence - as Alan Bennett puts it, one fucking thing after another - into a wholly new phenomenon. It was, I now understood, concerned with not *the* perception of reality, but *a* perception. It stretched not just backwards, but forwards, into my future.

***

I cultivated the habit of noting down odd items which caught my eye in books and old news items. In periods of high discipline these were meticulously recorded in wire-bound notebooks. But these periods of discipline were infrequent. Over the following years periods of high activity vied with oceans of doldrums. More often than not, items of information would be scribbled on whatever scrap of paper was to hand and would then, as if by magic, congregate in the backs of drawers or the pockets of seldom worn jackets from which they would be eventually retrieved for bewildered contemplation. Many was the time I would rediscover some cryptic note that clearly, with no shadow of doubt at some point in the past, held the key to the whole mystery but which was, now, indecipherable. From time to time I would indulge in a frenzy of ruthless housekeeping in which I would save only those notes that were not composed in Swahili. I found some surprises.

One day, while mulling over for the millionth time the unlikelihood of Rotherham's innocence, I came across a scrap of paper that told of the trial of two men, George

Bates and Joseph Lessayed, who had been brought before the assizes on a charge of burglary from which they netted the then princely sum of £10. They were brought up at 9.30 in the morning and, after a five hour trial, were found guilty and sentenced to death. They did not hang, their sentences being eventually commuted to life imprisonment.

A second, unrelated piece of paper told the story of a nameless man (a corner of the page was missing) tried for the theft of a cow, another crime that then attracted the underused but statutory death penalty. This, too, was commuted.

I had made notes of both stories around the time of my initial inquiries into the judicial system because they provided anecdotal information about the nature of crime and punishment in the early 19th Century. Then I looked again. The circuit judge presiding over the trial of the cattle thief was Sir John Bayley. The trial took place on July the 25th, 1817. In the case of Bates and Lessayed, again the judge was Bayley. Again heard on July 25th. The name Bates seemed familiar. I looked back through my notes and found the article that had appeared in the Nottingham Journal on August 2nd that year,

"The only capital cases were those of George Bates and Joseph Lees...."

Clearly the reporter had been either deaf, dyslexic or both. Lees was Lessayed. He and Bates were tried on the 25th of July, the trial beginning at 9.30 am and lasting till half past two in the afternoon. The man sentenced to death for the theft of the cow had been tried in the late afternoon of the same day.

But the 25th of July had been the very day Rotherham was tried. Despite the report that there had been two capital cases that day, there had in fact been three. Bates and

Lessayed/Lees were dealt with between 9.30 and 2.30. A five hour trial. The cattle thief case was heard in the *late* afternoon. It was clear, the trial of Charles Rotherham took place between these. At quite what time Regency man defined a July afternoon as becoming evening I'm not sure, nor do I know how long a break the judge and jury took for lunch. What does, however, seem abundantly clear from this is that sometime *after* 2.30 in the afternoon but *before* late afternoon, the court heard the case of Charles Rotherham. Fourteen witnesses were called. The jury deliberated and the judge passed sentence. I imagine it all took less than two hours to adjudicate on murder compared to the five afforded Messrs Lessayed and Bates for theft. Only two men were said to have hanged in Nottingham in 1817. Charles Rotherham was one of these, yet it seems Justice could only be seen to afford him a trial that lasted half as long as that allotted to deal with two men who stole £10.

The rush to judgement was conducted with obscene haste. Any reservations I might have been harbouring about the morality of preparing a belated defence for Rotherham were rapidly dispelled. Evidence which, on the face of it, had appeared damning now paled in the knowledge of the speed with which it was submitted. Charles Rotherham, whether innocent or guilty, was railroaded. But how? And why?

The original carved face of the memorial

to Bess, paid for and raised by the

gentlemen of Mansfield.

Richard Morley's refurbished inscription

with his correction to the spelling of Rotherham's

name.

Papplewick Church.

Bess lies to the left of the tower, by the sloped roof.

The ancient yew tree in Papplewick churchyard.

Grange Cottages where Bess lived

in the grounds of the now demolished

Robinson's Mill.

Linby churchyard.

To the foreground of this picture lie

the unmarked graves

of over 160 children who died in

Robinson's Mills.

The Seven Mile House.

Much changed since the early 19th century, this is where

Charles Rotherham is alleged to have stopped off

for refreshment.

Known then as the Ginger Beer House.

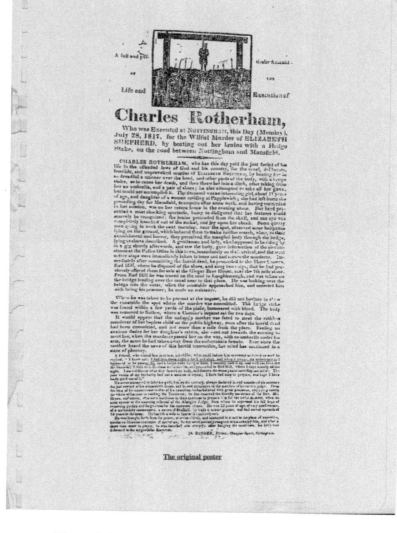

The original poster

The original 'penny dreadful' public coverage

of the crime.

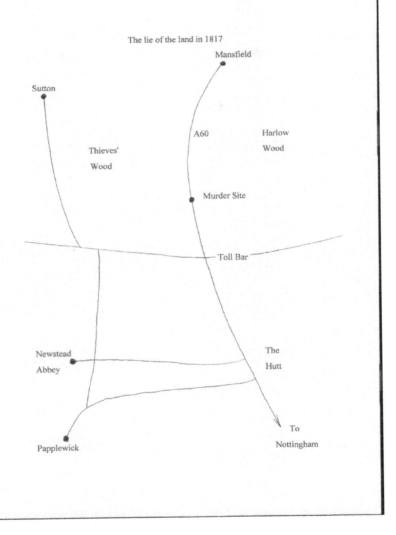

The lie of the land in 1817

Mansfield

Sutton

Harlow
Wood

A60

Thieves'
Wood

Murder Site

Toll Bar

Newstead
Abbey

The
Hutt

To
Nottingham

Papplewick

II

Seeking Bess
Defending Rotherham

There followed an interval of many months between my making the commitment to prepare Rotherham's defence and actually beginning it. Central to this delay was, again, the feeling that I was turning my back on Bess. It made no difference that I knew that what I was preparing to do for Rotherham was right, the disquiet remained. I was suspicious of my motives, perhaps seduced by the notion that there may be a deeper layer to the mystery - if indeed there *was* a mystery - than had ever been imagined. Was the temptation to go down this route less to do with some grand notion of Justice with a very large capital letter and more a latent tabloid appetite?

There is a profound sadness that surrounds Bessie Sheppard, one with which I am unlikely to ever come to terms. A loneliness, an isolation, in which time has imprisoned her. Despite the fact that my knowledge of her times had increased and that Regency Britain was daily unfolding before my eyes, Bess herself remained in shadow. There had to be something else that could be done. It was so wrong that a girl murdered in her sixteenth year should, in the relating of her own story, be once more marginalised.

There was only one way in which I could continue. It would take up much of my time and it would extend my involvement way beyond any I had ever envisaged. But it helped in that it freed me to defend Rotherham without the nagging guilt. I would, I decided, look for Bess.

At the time she died she had little past and no future. Maybe I could give her one. It was a strange idea but, though she was denied a future that July day, maybe one did not utterly perish with one's own demise. We all stand in a continuing parade. When I'm gone my children will carry with them in whichever way they see fit the echoes of my existence, In a way, I'll survive. Maybe Bess could, too? It was beyond anyone's power to hand back to her a full life, but maybe it was possible to pass on her memory, that warm

77

glow of belonging, to some family. If I could find them then maybe Bessie Sheppard had that same chance of being cherished, a chance she so deserved. Not only could I remove the isolation made so manifest by the stone by the roadside, maybe I could free her from the cul-de-sac into which history had shunted her.

This decision meant I could, with a clear conscience, begin my defence of Charles Rotherham. It had to be pursued in tandem with my search for Bess. Though it may not always be evident from the narrative that follows, this is what I did. All was concurrent. Any indication to the contrary can be attributed to the shortcomings of the writer.

***

The newcomer to genealogy entered a world of consummate confusion before the advent of Ancestry.com. and the like. If there was one lesson to be learned from my ramraid on history, it was that the volume of one's ignorance increases exponentially with the volume learned. Well, that and wait for computers to make it easier. You begin as a beginner and it's a status you can do little to shed.

I had no idea where to begin my search for Bess' family. What I did know of her was not, in itself, particularly helpful. She was single. She had, as far as I knew, no children. This clearly meant there would be no direct bloodline that I could conveniently follow from her down the generations. All I knew was that her mother was called Mary. I knew nothing of her father. He is never mentioned. What had become of him? Had he been caught up in the Luddite uprising? Had he wound up, like so many others, deported to the colonies? Perhaps he had gone with Wellington and, unlike Rotherham, died in battle? Or maybe he'd just abandoned his family and become a drunk.

I began to appreciate how much more difficult this new task was compared to the relatively easy searches I had had to make through the press of the day. Though that, at the outset, had seemed arduous, it in no way compared with the maze in which I now found myself. With news accounts it was a case of looking for the needle in the haystack. Now, before I could do anything, I had to find the bloody farmyard. As I understood the process, the normal way to build a family tree was to talk to the oldest surviving family member and work back. Frustrated from the outset, I had to do the exact reverse and no sign of Google.

***

Parish records contain details of the births, marriages and deaths of all but a few within their boundaries. The standard of care applied to their upkeep varies wildly, depending mainly upon the legibility of the vicar's handwriting, the volume of sherry imbibed on a Sunday afternoon and the conditions under which the many ledgers, once filled, were stored. Clearly those who completed the records had no inkling that they were in at the infancy of a soon to be billion dollar genealogy industry. Thankfully, with the increasing sophistication of technology, many records that would otherwise have perished, have survived and are freely available in libraries, public records offices and, lately, on the net.

Back then a session on a microfiche reader required, let me assure you, both preparation and not a little stamina. They are absorbing, they transport you to what you believe is a position where you will metaphorically peer through a window into the past. You will also, without noticing, likely starve to death. Take sandwiches - preferably in rustle-proof paper - and prepare to die.

The entry for Bess' burial was easy to locate in the records for Papplewick (and Linby). Her funeral was the only one conducted that day by Thomas Hurt. He misspells her name and gives her age as seventeen. The records, otherwise, are immaculate. Just a few years earlier, around 1800, they were much messier, the baptismal records crammed together on the page in what resembled a drunken sprawl. The ink is faded, making the deciphering of individual entries no easy task. Bess' name does not appear. In Sutton-in-Ashfield library I had access to the records for not just Papplewick and Sutton itself, but for Mansfield and a dozen or more surrounding villages. The next step was to make a thorough search of all parishes that bordered Papplewick, then to systematically increase the radius of that search. I met with no success. I accessed the records kept by the Mormon church (initially created in order that the Mormons could, post-mortem, baptize into their faith long dead relatives) but again without success. I was forced to conclude that Bess was either never embraced by any established religion or that she was baptized a Methodist. In either case, back then, I was lost.

For Charles Rotherham, similar enquiries would necessitate a trip to Sheffield. Having no knowledge of the city and, I must confess, a deep seated fear of driving into alien cities - being unable, as many people, to cope with the seemingly mundane task of finding a parking space - I adapted my approach to the search for his origins and launched a three pronged attack.

In those pre-internet days prong one was to write to the letters column in the Sheffield Star giving details of my quest. I hoped against hope that some descendant of Rotherham's might reply. Prong two was to scour the Sheffield phone book. This would have been a wonderful avenue of opportunity had Bess' killer been a Polish ex-patriot with a name composed entirely of consonants, but, for someone called after the next nearest big town it was like looking for a needle in a box of needles. Thirdly I could write to the Sheffield City Library to see if I could enlist their help.

Three months passed. In mid December a letter dropped onto the hall rug. The Sheffield archivist, one Kim Collis, had checked the parish records held there and found a Charles Rotherham who had been baptized at St Peter's church in Sheffield on the 27th of March, 1785, the son of Joseph and Ann Rotherham. Even better, on the 18th of November 1804 he had married one Ann Holmes in the same church and on June 17th, 1805, their son Joseph was born and baptized on July the 14th. Neither Charles nor his wife could write.

Kim Collis went on to inform me that they had searched for an apprentice indenture - as the Nottingham press had indicated may exist - but without success. It seemed likely it had been destroyed, but Kim referred me to the Public Record Office in Kew where, with luck, I might also find details of Rotherham's army service. I did as advised and wrote. Before long a bulky brown envelope dropped through the letterbox bearing a Kew postmark. From its bulk I concluded they must have traced a hell of a lot about Rotherham but, upon opening, a veritable rain forest's worth of glossy leaflets cascaded to the floor. The PRO, to my naive surprise, could not undertake private research but, were I to call, they would supply me with a reader's ticket and I could search myself. It didn't take me long to calculate that to find what I was looking for could take quite a while. With Christmas almost upon us I couldn't afford (nor, might I add, could I have afforded were Christmas not to be upon us) to spend money on what could turn out to be a wild goose chase. I put it from my mind. It would be years before I could afford the indulgence.

***

If Charles Rotherham was baptized, as Kim Collis had said he was, in 1785, then it's likely he was born very soon before. This may seem self-evident but experience has taught me it's not. In the parish records of the late Victorian era it is not uncommon to find details of mass baptisms of entire families. All the money earned by the head of the house had to go towards putting bread on the table. Baptisms, though desirable, weren't essential. In addition, whilst the birth rate was high, so was the mortality rate for infants. Common sense, therefore, decreed that families wait to ensure a child's survival before going to the expense of a baptism. Harsh, perhaps, but pragmatic.

By contrast, Regency parents tended not to delay the baptism, so it was reasonable to establish the rough time for Rotherham's birth. At the time of his marriage he would have been just twenty. The news accounts say he served with Wellington for twelve years through to 1815. He can have had little, if any, married life before going off to war.

I have read something of the war and of the battles in which he was engaged. Why, though, had he left his new bride so soon after marriage and perhaps before his son's birth to risk his life fighting the post-revolutionary French? Somehow I doubted it had much to do with some patriotic drive to either defend freedom or preserve the prosperity of his homeland - there was little trace of either for the likes of he.

He was apprentice to a scissor grinder. Trial reports said he had served all but his last year, presumably forgoing the trade to take the King's shilling. Food, we know, was at a premium. Wages were desperately low. People were, quite literally, starving. The staple food of the masses, according to JB Priestley in his book, "The Prince of Pleasure", was barely palatable bread, brown in colour due its having been made with contaminated flour, and potatoes, frequently rotten. Priestley suggests that the aversion to brown bread in the first half of the 20th Century was likely due to the class memory of what brown bread used to be - *dirty* bread.

Contrast this with the life of the aristocracy. The Prince Regent - the *de facto* king - held banquets at Windsor on tables two hundred yards long that groaned under the weight of every food imaginable borne upon plates of silver and gold. Beau Brummel, the infamous dandy and acquaintance of the Regent, was a frequent guest. He was a relatively conservative figure when set beside many of his contemporaries. Sir Lumley Skeffington, known affectionately as 'Skiffy', painted his face and bathed his body in heady perfumes. Henry Cope, of Brighton, the so called *Green Man* wore nothing that was not green. His rooms were green, as were his possessions. It's said he also never ate anything that wasn't green. It was a time of studied ostentation and decadence. An age of indulgence like few before or since, and at its core, both rotten and empty.

What must the poor have made of all this? Very little, to say the least. Riots stemming from hunger were commonplace. The war with France had deprived us of badly needed trade. We had, clumsily, lost the Americas. Official bungling had cost us the Isle of Corsica which, had it been retained, would have resulted in Bonaparte being an Englishman. Back home, a run of disastrous summers had depleted the grain harvest, pushing prices ever higher.

The picture was very, very bleak. The gulf between the haves and have-nots was vast and widening. The solution for many men was to enlist in the army in order to eat, food being a little more plentiful for the soldiers. They would readily enlist and depart for foreign climes where, not from any sense of duty but from an urgent need to fill an empty belly, they both risked, and surrendered, their lives. Under Wellington the forces were remarkably well disciplined considering the deprivation from which they were almost wholly drawn. The Infantry and the Artillery were particularly effective, their battle losses being light compared to those of the French. This was remarkable for some of the heavy cannon used first saw duty in the days of the Spanish Armada. The ammunition, too, did little to enhance their efficiency, it being a veritable mongrel of calibres, each painted a different colour to differentiate but in practice issued utterly arbitrarily to each weapon. Often the shot was so undersized that the rammer could insert, with ease, his hand between the shot and the barrel. At times the British were in much greater danger from misfires than they ever were from the muzzles of the enemy.

Whether the news reports at the time of Rotherham's trial with regard to his army service were accurate I never discovered, but they stated he saw action in numerous, horrific theatres of war. Conditions for the troops were appalling. Though food rations were adequate while still on British soil, they deteriorated rapidly upon embarkation. The Battle of Maida took place on the southernmost tip of Italy on July 4th, 1806. From then to his service in the Peninsular Wars in Spain and Portugal nothing is known, but in those wars the intensity of engagement with the enemy was high. In Spain alone he is said to have fought at Badajoz on April 6th, 1812; two months later, on June 19th he saw action at Ciudad Rodrigo and, but a month after on July 22nd, at Salamanca. From these battles the army marched north into France where, on April 10th, 1814, Rotherham fought at Toulouse. Here according to a participant in his diary, one Captain Wilson, he fought and suffered,

"...mud actually up to my middle..."

The trial report of Rotherham tells he saw out the whole of the campaign up to Waterloo without sustaining any wound. So did he take steps to avoid the fray? Reports of casualties from France and Spain indicate that Rotherham's feat was by no means unique. Many men, miraculously, returned from the conflict unscathed. Cowardice over such a lengthy campaign would inevitably resulted in execution. We must not judge Rotherham a coward. There is no evidence. Fear, I have no doubt, was his constant companion. But cowardice? I doubt it.

***

My lack of success in locating Bess' baptismal record presented me with a real, and possibly insurmountable, problem. To find any descendants I needed either a brother or a sister, preferably a brother who would carry the family name. For such records I really needed more information on the parents, but I knew nothing outside of her mother's name, Mary Sheppard.

Again the Papplewick records were my starting point, where once more I examined every marriage record. The plan was to examine those same records in every parish that bordered Papplewick, working on the theory that in the late 18th Century folk didn't move any further than they needed from their place of birth. It would necessitate checking the records of seven or eight parishes, located in two separate towns, just to accomplish one expansion of the boundary. If I met with no success that number would increase rapidly.

Once more in Angel Row, Nottingham among the pensioners and the school kids, I chose randomly my first parish of Bulwell. Long since absorbed by Greater Nottingham, but in Bess' day it was a separate village with its own identity. To both my great shock and delight, I hadn't been searching more than half an hour when I read, in barely legible, faded ink of the marriage on August the 8th,

85

1798, of Mary Bower and Charles Sheppard. Had it taken me longer to find I would have perhaps coped better with the success, but, so soon after the start, I was filled with doubt. Maybe there were a dozen or more Mary Sheppards lying around the pages of history waiting to deceive me. It wasn't, after all, *that* unusual a name. I checked, checked again and then re-checked. I went through the Mormon records. The marriage I had found was the only one recorded for a Mary Sheppard in the whole of Nottinghamshire within a period of ten years either way.

Of course, in isolation and even if this was the right couple, they were of no use to me unless they had had other children *and* they had disappeared from the Bulwell environs within a few years, thus enabling them to re-emerge in the Papplewick records. I studied the baptismal records from August 1798 onwards plus all other available records for Bulwell without a single recurrence of the Sheppard name. The very absence excited me. Surely this was, indeed, the Papplewick Sheppard family. I returned to Sutton where, in the library, I went through the baptismal log for Papplewick once more. How I had missed it on the other occasions I had been through, I don't know, but there, in black and white, was the entry that tied it all together, at least thus far.

On June the 12th, 1808, in Papplewick, a little boy was baptized. His name was Joseph Sheppard. His parents were shown as Charles and Mary Sheppard. Bess was not alone. She had a younger brother who, at the time of her murder, was just nine years old.

The relief I felt with this discovery was not just for me and my task, but for Mary in her grief. It helped to think that, throughout this terrible period, she had a son around whom she could wrap her arms for comfort. In that moment I knew that what I had set out to do was right and that, with luck, I might one day place Bess in a family's care.

***

While creating torment for the ordinary citizen seems to be the primary outcome of war, it also creates riches. By the planned exploitation of the resources of the poor, the young, the weak and the defenceless in order to procure arms, greedy entrepreneurs through the ages have ensured that sufficient wealth is creamed off to luxuriously line their own pockets. The wealth created in such circumstances is there today in the vaults of the old money families, though hands have long since been scrubbed clean and fortunes laundered into respectability. To such people the outbreak of peace was not good news. It interrupted their profitable pursuits. It was not they, however, who suffered. It's still the poor, the young, the weak, the defenceless. Without the benefits of war, it is they who must be made to bear the unavoidable burdens of increased unemployment, deepening consequential poverty and decay that moved forward with a new relentlessness.

Disease, we have seen, was rife - typhoid claimed many victims. The lack of a decent diet produced a population ill-equipped to withstand illness, a population that succumbed to pestilence. The chasm between rich and poor reached its widest and, as a result, civil unrest increased. Fear persisted in the minds of the aristocracy that revolution of the kind experienced in France was still a possibility. Such stirrings were to be quashed at all costs. The government made illegal *all* gatherings, however innocuous. By such means they could stifle even legitimate questioning of their policies, let alone uproot the weakest shoots of perceived rebellion. Justifiable pleas from the poor, if formulated by other than the individual standing alone, were considered to have emanated from hotbeds of subversion and were deemed treasonable. Habeas Corpus was suspended, making it legal to arrest and imprison, with or without trial and without even a discernible offence having been committed.

Vagrancy was outlawed - this with thousands of homeless soldiers returning - strangers being treated, without exception, as troublemakers.

The children who worked in the mills who hitherto had expected little more than the promise of an early grave were now, in this new, unwelcome peace, even more unwanted. Deprived of the meagre shelter afforded them under the auspices of the mill owners, they gravitated now to the *flash houses*, little more than doss houses that appeared in towns and cities, the prototypes of the Dickensian hovels that would later become so familiar; the homes of street urchins, aspiring pickpockets and infant prostitutes.

What could the kids do? What was the alternative? For the majority, dragged from the slums of London to become factory fodder, the only people to ever put value on their lives were the mill owners. Now they had no use for them. They were a drain on a shrinking pocket. At least the flash houses, for all their dangers, offered some meagre hope of survival in a world bent on their destruction. Survival, for some of the many children, meant selling their bodies to the fat Regency toffs.

Child prostitution was widespread in the late 18th Century, but now, with ever fewer means of survival, it thrived. Countless youngsters were swallowed by the insatiable market for juvenile flesh.

In the larger conurbations, the smallest children were employed as chimney sweeps, driven up the choking flues by cruel masters, often urged on their way by fires lit in the hearths below. Many frail, charred bodies were grudgingly removed from chimneys by disgruntled masters to whom the death of a child was no more than a costly hindrance.

Few gained from the peace. Few, that is, except for the soldier, no longer called upon to put his life on the line for so grateful a nation. Perhaps, as they waited patiently on the quaysides of France and Belgium for transport home, they looked upon themselves as heroes. Maybe they imagined themselves returning to welcoming crowds, to warm, open arms. Wellington, after romantic dalliances with Napoleon's own lovers, had returned to just such a hero's welcome. If he was a hero, so then are we, they must have believed. With high expectation they must have made that return trip across the channel. Among their number was Charles Rotherham, by then a thirty year old man, returning - or so he believed - to his wife and son, to a life. What he and his many comrades in arms found upon disembarking was not what they had expected.

In the absence of the film camera the immediacy of war, that we now take for granted, is lost. Not until the US conflict in Vietnam in the 1960s were television viewers afforded the dubious privilege of witnessing the equally dubious heroics of their troops. Now, with further technological advances, the theatre of war has been turned into a virtual video game with we, the viewers, embedded participants. After Vietnam and ensuing wars on foreign turf, right down to the removal of Saddam Hussein, no matter how vigorously politicians wave the flag, no matter what fine rhetoric they employ to convey how highly we value those who fought on our behalf, the fact is they return to very little. When the fervour dies there is little to replace it. The men are, and were, forgotten. Their minds scarred with the horrors of battle, we abandon them. Post-war economies leave many without a livelihood. The heroes of yesterday then, as now, become forgotten men.

Without modern media coverage, things were even worse in 1815. For those who remained on England's shores, the problems of survival in what was then their *modern* world, had never gone away. Heroes were expendable when the belly was empty. The thousands of ex-servicemen flooding back to England were just one more threat, one more problem. They had to eat - and there was little enough already. They needed work but that meant stealing food from already starving mouths.

Consider for a moment how the soldiers must have felt to find themselves face to face with the sudden realisation that, far from being heroes, they were considered parasites. After years during which they understood their function as part of a fighting machine, they now found they had no place, no role, no value. Exposed for so long to the harsh realities of warfare, the prospect of sudden and lingering death, they now had to contend with something far more insidious, the hatred of their fellow countrymen.

Many came back to find their marriages in tatters. Many loved ones would have in their absence perished in the pestilence which they had escaped. There would be little news received at the front. Charles Rotherham, after but the briefest taste of married life, could expect little. He had no trade, he had abandoned it to soldiering. As many others, he likely resorted to that universal panacea - the bottle. Drink and the nomadic life became the norm for many of these men, roaming the country seeking what work they could and then losing themselves to the oblivion of booze. What else, in all truth, was left for them? To what degree had they been fundamentally changed, irrevocably damaged, by their endurance of ten years of conflict?

It was to this England, this Sheffield, and ultimately, this Mansfield, that Charles Rotherham returned. It was this set of circumstances - tragic already even before the death of Bess - that led to the union of their names on July 17th, 1817. Two strangers who, but for a brutal few seconds, had no other connection the one with the other.....

***

90

With the existence of Joseph Sheppard established beyond doubt, I continued with my search for Bess' descendants with renewed optimism. Needless to say, he wasn't content with sitting tightly in Papplewick, marrying a local girl, raising a family and then gaining my attention. Things weren't to be *that* easy. However, had I known then what I was later to discover about the nomadic nature of my quarry, I would have savoured this leg of the quest for the picnic that it eventually proved to have been.

Joseph Sheppard was born around the middle of the first half of 1808 and baptized in June of that year. I began the long search for his later movements, for his marriage in the records of peripheral parishes for the years 1828/29. Logically it might have made more sense to check the burial records first as the possibility of premature death was high, but I didn't want to tempt fate (though quite how this could have worked retrospectively I never asked myself), - searching for his death might, incongruously, invite it.

Staring unproductively at images on microfilm can, after a few hours, create the same effect as having one's eyeballs sucked out by an industrial vacuum cleaner. This discomfort was sufficient to conjure up in my troubled mind less obvious scenarios which suddenly became threateningly plausible. What if Joseph was gay? Though statistically improbable I did plead with some greater being in whom I had no belief to just make him have had kids!

I exhausted the parishes up to the northern boundary of Nottingham (from whence his parents had come and to which, I thought, he may return) and moved elsewhere. It was within the precincts of my own home parish of, at that time, Sutton-in-Ashfield that I finally caught up with him. On leap year's day, the 29th of February, in the year 1832, Joseph married at the parish church. His bride, a widow of some ten years his senior, was one Elizabeth Eaton. Despite the success I continued my search finding no more Joseph

91

Sheppards around the right age or spelled in any of the various ways the surname could appear in any other parish or national record. I was happy I had my man.

Joseph's wife, Elizabeth, had first been the wife of John Eaton, marrying him in Mansfield on August 17th, 1822. With him she bore three children - James, Ruth and Elijah. John died, aged just 33, in 1829 and was buried on July 19th. Three years of widowhood ensued before she married our Joseph. Fingers crossed, I sought further children of the new marriage. Joe didn't let me down.

Just five months after the marriage they produced a son, Richard. With this nephew for Bess, I took the first step down the generations toward today. The isolation within which she had till now been confined was beginning to crumble...

***

The time had come to begin to prepare my defence of Charles Rotherham. What excuse was there for further delay? I'd made some faltering headway in the search for Bess' lineage which I told myself would assuage any guilt I might feel at defending her alleged killer. I understood a little of the pain central to Rotherham's life and something of the rejection he must have experienced upon his return to these shores after the war. So why still this reluctance to begin?

One cannot criticise in a reasonable manner the judicial system of another nation merely because the moral foundations upon which that system is based do not coincide precisely with our own. Likewise, one cannot look back into history and apply the same criteria employed today in determining guilt or innocence. As they say, the past is another country. The distance in social evolution is at least as great temporally as geographically. In defending Charles

92

Rotherham it would be insufficient for me to simply apply, retrospectively, the ploys of a contemporary defence to prove his innocence. You know, m'lud, the defendant was clearly suffering from post-traumatic stress disorder and was not responsible.... Moving goalposts to fix the result (valid though that might be) would just not be enough. I needed to establish reasonable doubt, but in an *absolute* manner. I would need to be sure that the defence I came up with would be, firstly, one which those present at the time could have produced were they to have bothered and secondly, one which would, were it to be presented to a jury of Rotherham's peers, (which didn't happen) give at least a chance of acquittal. That was the stumbling block. I couldn't allow myself to tinker with the past. Hell, it wouldn't make any difference anyway. He has been dead now almost two hundred years. I had to accept that failure was a possibility and that I would then have to live with the fact that he went to the gallows, at least by the standard of the times, justly.

I baulked. It felt like a game. It felt artificial. From the comfort of my armchair I was deliberating in an intense, yet utterly safe, manner. These were *real* people. All this *really* happened. What was it like to die choking on the gallows, in front of tens of thousands baying for your blood, iron shackles clanking at your ankles? What torments plagued Rotherham that last night in his death cell, the dampness of the air clinging to his skin like death itself, waiting in the blackness for the distant sound of the wagon that was to transport him to Gallows' Hill?

Did he focus on those first few moments when his neck succumbed after the drop or on the torment that awaited him? Was his life already at an end even before he heard the name Bessie Sheppard? Would the grip of the hemp around his crushed throat be the last blossom of pain before he went elsewhere? Did he have faith? I heard the sounds of iron on cobbles, the simmer of the anticipating crowd, the priest's disjointed words. The hood.

Humanity is on loan. It is not owned by the one or the many. It accidentally transcends time, a minute ripple in a still, boundless pool. Given the different beat of a distant butterfly's wing, I could have been Charles Rotherham.

In something like anger, I began.

***

The chronology of events for July 1817 was this:

7 July - The murder of Bess.

8 July - The arrest of Rotherham.

9 July - The Coroner's Inquest.

10 July - Bess' buried at Papplewick.

14 July - Rotherham arraigned at Sutton-in-Ashfield.

25 July - The Trial.

28 July - The Execution.

29 July - Rotherham buried in an unmarked grave.

The sole new fact added to the above timetable was Rotherham's appearance at the Coroner's Court. The Nottingham Journal, 19th July, reports:

The Coroner's Jury met at Sutton-in-Ashfield on Monday last before Thomas Wright, Gent, Coroner, for the further investigation of the horrid murder mentioned in our journal when the verdict of wilful murder was given against Charles (not William) Rotherham, who was by the said Coroner committed to the county gaol for trial at the ensuing assizes.

I made enquiries of the Nottingham County archive, but no verbatim record of the hearing exists, nor is there any surviving documentation relating to the inquest held at the Blue Bell Inn in Sutton. I had all I was going to get. Here, in summary, was what I had gleaned from my sources.

At around noon on Monday the 7th of July, Elizabeth Sheppard, wearing new shoes recently made for her and carrying a borrowed umbrella, left her mother's house near the old Robinson Mill in Papplewick to walk to Mansfield where she was after a job. What happened there is not recorded but, according to Sarah Clay, she left the town at 5.57pm.

Three miles out of Mansfield she was attacked by Charles Rotherham who, according to witnesses, had been either following her or simply travelling the same route. In the ensuing fight, Elizabeth was battered to death with a hedgestake and her body tossed into a nearby ditch. Rotherham resumed his intended route to Nottingham.

Some fifteen minutes before Elizabeth left Mansfield, her mother, Mary, left the Papplewick cottage to meet her as she was, by this time, worried. She walked to the same toll bar toward which Rotherham was headed. Between the toll bar and the Hutt, Rotherham and Mary crossed paths. Mary then waited at the toll bar while Rotherham, having just met an ex-soldier called William Ball, went into the Hutt for a drink. Soon after, though it's not known exactly when, Mary returned home.

After the drink with Ball, Rotherham continued on his journey to Nottingham, stopping briefly for a soft drink at the Ginger Beer House a few miles further on, then moving on to the Three Crowns at Red Hill where he spent the night after trying to sell Bess' shoes.

95

Next morning, Tuesday the 8th, Bess' body was found by quarrymen on their way to work at 6.15am. The Mansfield and Nottingham authorities were alerted. That same morning, Rotherham left the Three Crowns without the shoes and went on to Nottingham. Again there's a blank when he's in the city and he next emerges at the Rancliffe Arms in the little village of Bunny, where he now tried to sell the umbrella.

Ben Barnes, a Nottingham constable, began his search. Hearing of the reported sighting in Bunny, he set off in pursuit. Rotherham was arrested in the afternoon of the 8th on a bridge about a mile north of the town of Loughborough. He was taken by Barnes (and his colleague Linneker) to Nottingham gaol beneath the Shire Hall.

On Wednesday the 9th, Barnes took him to Sutton to appear at the Coroner's Court held in the Blue Bell Inn. There he was charged with the murder of Bessie Sheppard. The inn was besieged by locals who wanted to look at him. Barnes did his best to keep the crowd at bay but Rotherham insisted they be allowed to see him.

Barnes then took Rotherham back to Nottingham, on which journey he is said to have pointed out to Barnes where he had found the hedgestake. He told him he had no idea why he killed her. He denied any attempt at rape.

Rotherham was held in the gaol until his trial on July the 25th, a Friday. Following a guilty verdict he was held till Monday the 28th, when he was hanged on Gallows' Hill in Nottingham and subsequently buried in an unmarked grave within the precincts of St Mary's Church, Nottingham, across the road from the court.

That was the story. A few things immediately bothered me. Firstly, the speed of Rotherham's arrest so far from the scene of the crime. Secondly, anomalies thrown up by the various reports. For instance, Barnes said he took Rotherham to Sutton on the Wednesday. Were he to be charged with murder at that court, on the 14th, then the Wednesday in question was the 9th, the day after the arrest. The Nottingham Review of the 11th reports:

'....a coroner's inquest sat on Wednesday (the 9th), but no verdict was pronounced, the proceedings being adjourned to this day (the 11th)....on account of the impracticability of getting witnesses from such different and distant parts.'

These *different and distant* parts, it would seem from the list of witnesses presented at the trial, were mainly Mansfield, the adjoining town.

So why the delay? What could have happened to Rotherham while in Ben Barnes' custody (it was Barnes, after all, who tried to keep the crowds back from the Blue Bell) between the 9th, when taken from the county gaol, and the 14th, when he was charged with the murder.

Was there any truth in the story that Mary Sheppard, Bess' mother, met Rotherham on the road soon after the murder?

The thread that linked all these things was *time*. The brief time taken to catch Charles Rotherham. The time unaccounted for in his journeys to and from Sutton and the irony of time's apparent conspiracy in ensuring the dead girl's mother passed her killer face to face.

Benjamin Barnes interested me greatly. Leaving aside Rotherham's alleged confession, so much of Barnes' evidence was instrumental in delivering Rotherham to the hangman. Much was hearsay, what Rotherham was said to have said but which none in that court heard him say for he never spoke. They were quite content to hear second hand testimony, despite the presence of the man responsible right there in court!

97

So, where do I begin? If, as it appeared, time was of the essence, it might be fruitful to try to replicate the last journey of Bessie Sheppard.

**

The least of my problems in reconstructing Bess' last walk was the casting of characters. My wife at the time, Lynne, had taken an interest in the story from the beginning. Perhaps it was a fair indictment of the social whirl she had found herself in being married to me, but she jumped at the chance to play the part of a murder victim's mum one cold, damp Sunday morning.

The plan was this. I would drive to Papplewick, drop her outside the Sheppard's cottage, then go on to Mansfield from whence we would both set out at pre-determined times (there were no mobile phones) based upon the evidence given by Sarah Clay and Mary Sheppard. She along Mary's route, myself playing Bess. We would try to maintain a steady pace without any contrivance to make the slower progress likely in 1817 and would time ourselves between set locations. Any allowance for conditions would be possible later mathematically.

It was the 19th of August, 1990, at a quarter past nine in the morning, following the synchronisation of watches that we set out, Lynne with a slightly bewildered air of amusement at this novel manifestation of conjugal rights.

There were, clearly, obvious differences between this journey in 1990 and that of Bess and Mary in 1817. We would enjoy proper pavements, in 1817 tarmac had not reached Mansfield. The Nottingham road would be deeply rutted by the wheels of coaches that regularly plied it. The weather for July, according to reports I was able to trace, told of severe hailstorms as recent as the 5th. Crops had been flattened, houses struck by lightning. Rainfall for the

98

month was almost six inches. In bad weather the rutting of the roads could render them little more than rivers. Indeed, having gone equipped with a borrowed umbrella, Bess clearly expected the worst.

Aside from conditions underfoot, we also had the advantage of modern footwear. Bess wore new shoes, even today notoriously uncomfortable. Rotherham would likely still be shod in his old army boots. He would have the benefit of being accustomed to a hard slog over bad ground, having experienced no casual stroll through the Iberian peninsula, but we, I was convinced, still had the edge.

What of our physical condition? I, for one, had had a good breakfast after a sound night's sleep. Rotherham, it's said, had just consumed seven pints of beer before leaving Mansfield. Though the potency of ale at the time might vary, due to the same mashing of hops being used for multiple brews, I very much doubt it was any less toxic than seven pints of today's homogenised refreshment. Maybe, during the day, Bess had consumed a few cold potatoes or some bread and cheese wrapped for her by her mother. Maybe she had eaten nothing. In the book, 'Poverty and the Industrial Revolution' (Inglis,1971) the ruling classes made their suggestions to the masses. They recommended, it said, boiling an ox head with peas and oatmeal for three and a half hours as an alternative to the salty bacon consumed by many.

I left Mansfield at three minutes to ten, mimicking Bess' departure at 17.57. My starting point was close to the church of St Peter, the only church at that time to have a clock face (iPhones being at a premium) and be near to the mill in which Sarah Clay, the girl who supplied Bess' departure time in court, worked. Why, I had wondered, would Sarah supply so accurate a time? Wouldn't it be normal to recall it as being, at best, *around six*? Had something happened that gave Sarah cause to remember Bess' leaving time so well, and if so, why had we not been told what this thing was? Had Sarah's observation of Bess been casual, or had she in fact been with her some considerable time? Would I, I asked myself, remember so precisely the time of an otherwise unmemorable occurrence? Or had, perhaps, Bess been in Sarah's company and quite suddenly become aware of the lateness of the hour, maybe remarking on the fact that her mother had been expecting her home considerably earlier? Mary, remember, was anxious about Bess and had set off to meet her, and this had been some fifteen minutes *before* Bess had even left Mansfield. What was it that could have detained Bess? These thoughts and more occupied me as I walked from town. On my left I passed what were, in Bess' days, the Water Meadows, not half a mile from my starting point. Back then this area of rough pastureland, through which meandered the River Maun, would have marked the southern boundary of the town. The road thereafter would have opened onto countryside. Today, though this same tract of land has long since been renamed Titchfield Park, alongside it is a modern swimming bath named, appropriately, Water Meadows. The road dipped. I left the built up area behind and headed toward the Forestry Commission plantation. Passing the crest of the hill I looked down the long, gradual decline to Rainworth water, locally said to be the site of Robin Hood's initial meeting with Friar Tuck. Just beyond the brow of the far hill lies Blidworth, from where Maid Marion is said by some to come and where Will Scarlet is reputedly buried.

As I neared the Sheppard stone I saw Lynne approaching down the long, yawning curve that reached down to the murder site from the one time location of the toll bar. We had covered the total distance of 7.2 miles and, when later measured by car, met almost at the midpoint, meaning we had, as intended, maintained a similar pace. The walk took one hour and fifty-three minutes over which we averaged 3.82mph.

The precise times Lynne and I recorded for the various stages were:

Mansfield to murder site - 48 minutes.

Murder site to toll bar - 10 minutes.

Toll bar to Papplewick turn-off - 18 minutes.

Junction to Bess' home - 37 minutes

This was much too fast for 1817, but using them as base times I could make arithmetical adjustments to produce a whole range of timings that might have been more suitable for then.

It was possible to take these times for sections of the walk and vary them, increasing them by between 10% and 50% over those actually taken. These could then be used to produce putative actual times at which events may have occurred.   For an example, had the three been able to average 2.7mph (30% slower than the speed we sustained) then Bess' journey from Mansfield would have taken her 63 minutes to reach the murder site at around 7.00pm. Had the murder been committed instantly, Rotherham would have reached the Toll Bar at 7.13pm after a walk of 13 minutes.

Mary Sheppard left Papplewick at 5.45pm. At 6.34 she would have arrived at the junction with Nottingham Road. A further 24 minutes would have brought her to the Toll Bar at 6.58, some fifteen minutes before Rotherham. In this scenario, the two would not have met. But how accurate could I be?

William Thompson, returning from Nottingham that evening, said that he saw the prisoner about a mile from where the murder was done and on the Mansfield side of it. This was between six and seven in the evening. Bess, he said, was some two or three hundred yards behind

Rotherham, walking in the same direction. He was, sadly, no more precise.

Thomas Highgate was returning from a Commissioner's meeting in Red Hill on the evening of the 7th, he said he passed Rotherham *at about seven o'clock* at a point halfway between the toll bar and the murder site. He estimated himself to have been about a third of a mile from where Bess' body was found next day. Measurements I made later proved his estimate to be commendably accurate.

So, if Charles Rotherham was indeed there at seven o'clock, what could this mean for the other timings? Would it be possible to pinpoint the time of the murder?

If Thomas Highgate was correct in his estimate for the time he saw Rotherham, and Rotherham had left town at about the same time as Bess, then Rotherham had by then walked some three and a half miles from the centre of town in sixty-three minutes. A speed of around 3.3mph - a remarkable rate.

If Rotherham, however, left before Bess (which is certainly possible bearing in mind Thompson's testimony that he was ahead of Bess) then Rotherham could have walked much more slowly, at a pace more in keeping with conditions underfoot.

The evidence of witnesses like Thompson and Highgate can be deceptive. One is not presented with a narrative account of a sequence of events, just snapshots. It would be wrong to draw any conclusions based upon these. It would be wrong to conclude that, because Thompson saw Bess behind Rotherham, that she was gaining on him. At the time Thompson says he saw them Bess may not have been catching him up, he may have already passed her. If that was the case, what stopped him striking at the first opportunity? Can we accept that this man, who was supposedly possessed of irrational desires at the moment of the murder, was bereft of those desires just minutes before when he passed her? If he passed her.

Let's examine the scenario suggested by Highgate's testimony a little more. If Bess left Mansfield at 5.57pm and Rotherham, whipping along at 3.3mph, was seen by Highgate at 7.00pm, then, by arithmetic manipulation of their speeds, he had walked for some six minutes after the murder. To maintain this considerable speed the murder would need to have been committed, literally, on the hoof, with no time to even break step. The time for the murder would, in this instance, have been set at 6.54pm, with Bess having cruised out of Mansfield at around 3.26mph. This speed difference between them allows for a gain of just 70 yards in an hour's walking. When Thompson alleges he saw them, just two miles into the walk, Rotherham was said to have been some two to three hundred yards ahead of her. Yet in the time they had been walking at speeds necessary to support Highgate's testimony, had they left Mansfield together, he had only time to gain some forty yards on her.

The only way whereby Rotherham could have been such a distance ahead of Bess by the time they were seen by Thompson was if Bess had rested briefly and for Rotherham to have passed her. She'd had a long day. What she had been doing during the day is unrecorded. It was said she had been successful in her search for work, yet no-one, oddly, came forward to substantiate this.

Rotherham could have left town well after her in this version of events. He would have had ample time to assess the situation as he approached her and to plan his moves before succumbing to temptation. *But he did not.* The murder took place further down the road. It had to have done. Rotherham was seen *ahead* of her. He had successfully, it seems, been able to rein in the passions aroused in him, only shortly thereafter to fail and witness them overcome him in sudden, bloody slaughter.

Discussion of whether Rotherham was in front of or behind Bess may seem unnecessarily pedantic. She was murdered. Fact. Well, yes. But we find here one of the contradictions of the case. Supposed testimony seems to vary. The Nottingham Journal records Ben Barnes, the police officer, testifying that,

"...he passed her without taking any particular notice, and proceeded on, till feeling himself weary, he sat down by the road to rest. Just as the young woman came up, the horrid idea entered his mind of murdering her...."

But the Review gives this version of what Barnes said,

"....he could not tell what possessed him at that moment, he never spoke to the woman, but the moment he got up to her, he struck her on the head and repeated his blows till she was lifeless...."

At no time did we get to hear Rotherham's own version of events. We are only told of the conversations he allegedly had with Ben Barnes. In the early 19th century the accused had the right to tell the court what had happened. Indeed, the simple fact that the court had insisted Rotherham plead not guilty seemed to suggest it wanted to hear the whole, sorry saga. Rotherham seemed to have no reluctance in confessing his crime, according to others, but in court he said nothing even though he had nothing to gain from silence.

So why was this silence maintained? Was Justice, in fact, the prime concern of the court, or was it more concerned with implanting the fear of God into the people following the unsettling times of late? You see, with a man so seemingly ready to confess his crime at any opportunity, why did he not do so in court? Or did they really not want to risk it? We had the hearsay. That was surely good enough.

104

Might there be a danger that Rotherham might tell a different story? Might he have said he didn't remember what he had done? He was drunk. But that would contradict the other evidence given by Ben Barnes to the effect that Rotherham had explained from exactly where he had taken the hedgestake.

Such thoughts are pure conjecture, but not without some foundation. You see, there were *two* police officers involved in this investigation and arrest. Ben Barnes and officer Linneker. Why was Linneker never called to give evidence? Surely he, too, heard Rotherham's confession? He had accompanied Barnes and the accused back from Loughborough. Was it to save court time? Surely not, they were milking this appearance. They had called the Sutton parish constable to give virtually a duplicate gory account of the hedgestake and the body.

Maybe Linneker was not called because he may have said that on the journey back from Loughborough he had never once heard Rotherham confess.

***

The third reference to times in the court case was in the evidence of Robert Cheadle, patron of the Three Crowns pub in Red Hill. According to reports in the Journal he had been in the pub in the evening of the 7th of July when Rotherham arrived there at nine-thirty. Red Hill is 9.5 miles from Mansfield, six miles on from where Highgate said he saw Rotherham at 7.00pm. Rotherham therefore covered this six miles in two and a half hours. He had made two stops for drinks. One at The Hutt where William Ball testified he had spent fifteen minutes with him taking a cup of ale. Rotherham had two pints according to the Journal - say thirty minutes. At the Ginger Beer House he stopped again for peppermint. Fifteen minutes? This leaves

105

Rotherham just an hour and three quarters to reach the Three Crowns where he stayed the night. This timing requires a walking speed of 3.4mph - close to the estimate for the earlier part of his journey of 3.3mph. If account is taken of the fact that Rotherham's journey was allegedly interrupted by his slaying of Bess, it can be seen that his speed throughout would have been around 3.4 mph. Was this possible? It's a healthy speed by modern standards and, as we can reasonably surmise, Rotherham was drunk and tired. He had, according to Cheadle, walked thirty-six miles that day. He was, however, fit, having endured similar feats of endurance under Wellington on the Iberian peninsula. Walking was the only means of getting about for the poor. They were accustomed to it, Rotherham probably more than most.

I concluded, in the face of common sense and arithmetic, that such a pace was possible for Rotherham. If so, then it is likely that Thompson passed Rotherham and Bess at 6.34pm - fitting in well with the evidence of the meeting as *between six and seven*. Rotherham would have been at the Toll Bar at 7.08 and at The Hutt a few minutes later. Assuming he didn't meet Ball until he had passed The Hutt, he would have reached the junction with the Papplewick road at 7.28. It's unlikely he got that far. I suspect he met Ball near to The Hutt at about 7.15.

The implications here are that, if Mary Sheppard left home at 5.45pm and if she was to have passed Rotherham, she would have had to have been at The Hutt at around the time that Rotherham was at the Toll Bar, that is 7.08. To cover the 3.1 miles of her journey she would have had to have maintained a speed of just 2.3mph. Mary is described in reports as having been anxious. I suggest a more accurate description might well have been, at the time, mad as fire. Hadn't Bess disobeyed her? Wasn't her mind filled with images of an uncaring daughter living it up (as far as such a thing was possible in the Mansfield of 1817 - not to mention 2014) in town? Mary, I suggest, moved a whole lot quicker than the maths suggest. I think she would have reached The Hutt just after a quarter to seven and would have been at the Toll Bar a little past ten to the hour. Rotherham didn't get there till 7.08. Had Mary waited at the Toll Bar for fifteen minutes (and in evidence this was never suggested) she would still not have passed Rotherham.

The story of Mary meeting her daughter's killer is, I believe, apocryphal. No more or less than an invention of the press. What I believe may well have happened, if my estimates are anywhere near accurate, is that Mary Sheppard stood at the Toll Bar at almost the very instant that her daughter - just out of sight around the distant bend, her shout swallowed by the thickets of trees - died.

Bessie Sheppard, I believe, died at eight minutes to seven on the evening of July the 7th, 1817.........

***

The search through the archives continued. When we left the Sheppards in the 1830s, Richard had just been born to Bess' younger brother Joseph and his new wife, Elizabeth. Richard was baptized on July the 25th, 1832. Joseph, at just 24 years of age, was the father of his own child and step-father to the three Eaton offspring aged 5, 7 and 9. Quite a burden for one so young.

It was four years before they produced any more children when, in 1836, they had another son, Charles, named after Joseph's father. Two years later, on July the 18th, 1838, a daughter came on the scene. Another Elizabeth, born, ironically, just twenty-one years to the day after her aunt's body was dragged from the ditch on Nottingham Road.

With each new child the scope for my search, and with it my optimism, increased. With three blood links established, surely I'd find my way to the next generation, then on, over the boundary into the twentieth century. Perhaps I'd be able to trace descendants within the memory of living people. The distance between Bess and I was decreasing. I wondered, were I ever to find them, if they would be aware of her? I longed to hand over her story to some member of a surviving family. Kind of, "here she is, cherish her."

Of the three children of Joseph and Elizabeth's union, it was Richard who took me a stage further. On October the 31st, 1853, Richard married. He and his bride, Eliza, wed at St. Peter's church in Mansfield.

It's strange how a sense of loss permeated my quest from time to time. Clearly everyone concerned had long since died, but, while searching for Richard's wedding in the records of this particular parish I found, on the 14th of May, 1854, just seven months after the marriage of his son Richard, the burial of Joseph Sheppard. He was forty six. He had survived Bess by thirty-six years and for the second time in her life his wife Elizabeth found herself a widow. She lived just two years longer, being buried beside him on July 13th, 1856, aged fifty-eight.

It was just two years between my learning of Joseph's existence and reading of his death. In those two years he lived in my imagination. He was not simply a name in a public record. He was - still is - the key to the door through which I would hopefully be able to carry his sister's memory. Joseph was *real*. I think of him with affection.

It is perhaps a timely warning to those who delve into the past to understand that time moves differently. Those whom we would wish to have loved are given to us and taken away with heartless rapidity. The joy of birth is quickly supplanted by the sorrow of death, with barely a hint of the breath in between that was life. Such brushes with the brevity of life affected me. To witness so often human life

108

reduced to nothing but entries on a page, mere punctuation marks in history, did not fill me as I might perhaps have expected it to, with a sense of pointlessness. Quite the reverse. I began to look around me and see life as a time in which one must seek the good, not the evil. The beautiful, not the beast. Hope, not despair. I never anticipated that I would owe a debt like this to Bess. Had she not died I would never have embarked upon this search. I would have left it for others to write these words, feel these feelings, think this thoughts. My life, a little because of Bess, passes more easily.

**

Things seemed at last to be beginning to move. I pressed on. Searching through the records for the children of Richard and Eliza I soon came across their first born. A daughter, Harriet, baptized on August 25th, 1855. Beyond that, however, there was nothing. Had she moved away? Perhaps died? I tried the Mormon index, burial records. Nothing. Was this the end? Was the line to disappear with Harriet? A barren period followed through which I truly believed my enquiries had ground to a bitter halt. Many were the times I distrusted my results, many the times I returned to check and double check. It was time consuming and fragile. Maybe, I'd tell myself, I'd just missed something. It wouldn't be unusual. I was proficient at missing things. I'd done the same thing with Joseph for so long. Perhaps inadvertently I'd skipped an acetate of records in my haste? Such desperate hopes kept me going when what I really felt was, if not quite despair, then certainly intense frustration. The tracks were fading.

It was months later, while flicking randomly through the microfilm, that my eye was caught by the record of a marriage on February the 26th, 1887, at St. Peter's church, Mansfield, the same place Richard had wed. On that day a Hetty Sheppard had married one William Dickinson. Both at the time were said to be living on Newgate Lane in Mansfield. It was the name of the father that particularly excited me. Richard Sheppard. He was described as a framework knitter, the same trade as Joseph. At the foot of the marriage record were the names of the witnesses to the union. Not just *Richard* Sheppard, but another *Elizabeth.*

With renewed enthusiasm I riffled through my papers. At the time of Richard's marriage he had been living on Ratcliffe Gate in Mansfield. Thirty years later, at the time of her marriage, the address of Hetty Sheppard was Newgate Lane. Newgate Lane runs off Ratcliffe Gate. Was this Hetty another daughter? Hetty was twenty-two when she married Dickinson. Her year of birth would have been around 1865 - ten years after Harriet. Small wonder, with such a gap, that I'd had trouble locating her if indeed she was who I was after. Still doubtful of my good fortune, I compared signatures on the marriage certificate of Richard and Eliza with those on Hetty's. In 1853 Eliza couldn't sign her name, but Richard could. The comparison of the two signatures of Richard Sheppard, written thirty-four years apart, revealed they were likely both by the hand of the same man. The convoluted *R*, the loops on the uprights, the accentuated *P*, the way in which the first letter of the surname linked to the following *h*, the shape of the script, all convinced me - along with the proximity of the addresses and the trades - that this Richard Sheppard was *my* Richard Sheppard.

Much later I was to learn, from sources which I could never have envisaged in my wildest dreams, much more of Richard Sheppard. What I learned went some considerable way to explaining some of the oddities that seemed to surround him.

I returned once more to the archives, hoping to satisfy myself beyond doubt that Hetty was indeed the daughter of Richard, Bess' nephew. Painstakingly I checked every single acetate sheet, every microfilm record for every Mansfield church and every surrounding parish. I inspected every baptismal record I could lay my hands on for every faith I knew and some I did not. I compared witness signatures and addresses. It was an arduous task, but necessary. In philosophy and logic there is a procedure known as *reductio ad absurdum*. It's kind of a posh version of 'if it looks like a duck and walks like a duck, it's probably a duck'. What it endeavours to do is to eradicate every other solution for a problem leaving just the one which, no matter how odd, has to be correct. I employed this device to satisfy myself that there was no other Richard Sheppard around at the time who could fit my bill but for the one who was the son of Joseph, the husband one time of Eliza and the father of both Harriet and Hetty.

Richard was a tragic figure. Harriet had not been his and Eliza's first child. Not five weeks after their marriage, on December the 4th, 1853, they buried their baby daughter, another Elizabeth, at just two weeks old.

Nine short months after Harriet's birth, Richard once more stood by the graveside, this time, on May 13th, 1856, of his wife Eliza. She was 25 years old. What happened after this second tragedy I did not then know. I searched for a re-marriage, hoping that through it he would find some peace. I found nothing. But Hetty had to have a mother. There was a gap in Richard's life I was, at that juncture, unable to fill. Quite how great a pain it must have been for him I did not fully appreciate. Events were deepening around me like the January snow outside. At times I was overwhelmed by the drifting, often blind to the individual flakes. Taking a little time to review the Richard I was coming to know, flicking back through the reams of notes that comprised just a portion of the jigsaw of his life, what emerged was a picture of devastating, almost unbearable sadness. In less than three short years, between October 1853 and July 1856, Richard mourned four of those closest to him. In December '53 he buried his daughter Elizabeth. Five months later, in May '54, he laid his father Joseph to rest. Fifteen months after this, in August '55, his wife gave him a daughter Harriet. Things he must have hoped, were looking up. But no. When baby Harriet was just nine months old, his wife died at twenty-five. As if that were not enough, two months later his mother Elizabeth was buried. Had it not been for Harriet, eleven months old at the end of this cycle of grief, Richard Sheppard would have been utterly alone in the world.

Modern psychologists measure trauma and stress by reference to life crises. Such crises are not exclusively negative experiences. Both marriage and the birth of children figure prominently in the list. By such criteria, Richard Sheppard underwent six crises within the space of thirty-three months. The cumulative effect of these would have destroyed less resilient and resourceful men. Richard had to fight to survive. Maybe - and this would be readily understandable were it to have been the case - he made fundamental changes in his life, changes designed to free him from some of the pain with which he had been afflicted. At the time I knew nothing of these changes. Someone later, thousands of miles away, provided me unknowingly with some of the answers.

Soon after his mother's death Richard took some solace in drink. It was not enough. To submerge himself in the bottle was a temporary solution. Richard was a bright, intelligent man. He turned to music, joining a roving band of madrigal players who travelled the land by horse and cart staging performances wherever they could find an audience. At some point during this revitalisation of Richard Sheppard, he found himself a new partner. Whether he re-married or not I have no idea. What is, however, clear is that, by the time he returned to Mansfield on a permanent basis he had three daughters. Harriet, Hetty and - do I really need to say - Elizabeth!

It was *this* Elizabeth, born around 1868, who was the second witness, along with Richard himself, at the wedding of Hetty Sheppard and William Dickinson. How can I be sure? Well, Elizabeth Sheppard Jnr. was herself married on April the 8th, 1890, to a man named Waldron. The witness signature on Hetty's marriage certificate corresponds exactly with that of Elizabeth's at her own wedding.

The lady, Hetty Dickinson, nee Sheppard, became the focal point of my search. Though with the absence of sons I had come to the end of the Sheppard name, I was soon to be exhilarated by the new and unexpected directions in which Hetty took me. To lands from which, many thousands of miles away, I was to learn of events on my own doorstep.

***

Clearly, one insurmountable problem in casting doubt upon the guilt of a man hanged, as I write this, near two hundred years ago is the fact that, by the time the pen is belatedly lifted in his defence, not only the condemned man but the witnesses too have long occupied their silent graves. Without access to these people the trial reports, far from shedding light on the truth, just cast more shadows. So many questions, it seemed, were doomed never to receive answers.

I said earlier that in the investigation of past crime one must take great care not to employ too readily modern perceptions of justice in order to condemn the deliberations of those whom, in all good faith, just did the best they could. One is compelled, however, to consider the innate fragility of such systems. Though the decisions of the courts may have been valid at the time in the absence of investigative sophistication, we must take care not to overcompensate for our smug superiority by viewing them, almost patronisingly so, with a benevolence that they really don't deserve. In any legal system, at any time in history, there are, on top of any inherent shortcomings, pressures brought to bear by both the Judiciary and the public alike to deliver verdicts that society, often at its most vengeful, demands. Such moods exist regardless of the distance down which a society believes itself to have travelled on the road to civilisation.

We know today of numerous cases where vital evidence has been, if not wholly suppressed, then certainly concealed from the defence if that evidence had a tendency to acquit. Evidence has been tampered with in a material way or, more frequently, highlighted in a way that leads a jury in the direction that the forces of law and order would have them proceed to strengthen those prejudices they assume society holds. Belated reviews of miscarriages of justice have resulted in many verdicts being found unsafe. Official corruption has, over the years, condemned many innocent men to languish in a prison cell. Human nature will always tend, in the absence of any political will to prevent it, to render any system corrupt. The practice is timeless. It is just the degree of the ensuing tragedy that varies.

In Britain prior to the abolition of capital punishment in the 1960s, we hanged men whom we knew to be innocent. Men who should never have been hanged if the contemporary understanding of justice had been honestly applied. Derek Bentley was one such victim. Hanged in the 1950s for his part in the shooting of a policeman, Bentley never fired a gun. He could not. He was both unarmed and under arrest at the time. Nevertheless the system demanded not justice, but revenge, and Bentley hanged for allegedly having uttered the words,

"Let him have it Chris."

114

The prosecution argued that Bentley was inciting his accomplice, Chris Craig, to murder and was therefore as guilty of the deed as Craig, who was too young for the gallows. Many at the time, with considerable justification, argued that Bentley was urging Craig to surrender the gun. Police evidence, much of which was curiously withheld, suggested Bentley possibly never even uttered the words that were deemed sufficient to secure his execution. Derek Bentley hanged. The Appeal Courts and the Home Secretary of the day closed ranks. Bentley had to die *to encourage the others*. Not my words; theirs.

Derek Bentley was educationally subnormal. He suffered from epilepsy and was defined by expert witnesses as, clinically, a moron. History has since learned that, far from being the dangerous criminal the authorities would have had us believe he was, Bentley was a kind, gentle, harmless kid. Some forty years after his execution he was granted a Queen's pardon.

I make this brief digression simply to illustrate the fact that, even with past crime, one cannot safely argue that justice is a variable commodity linked to its time and that verdicts reached, though perhaps anathema today, were then wholly justified. Judicial and political expediency all too frequently stifles truth. Fairness, rightness, compassion, justice. These are absolute concepts. The state, it's said, chose two thousand odd years ago to execute someone called Jesus Christ. Of somewhat less renown, but no less dead, is Derek Bentley, whom the state also chose to kill. It may have exercised a similar prerogative with Charles Rotherham.

***

Central to Rotherham's case was a question of identification. Two crucial witnesses, Thomas Highgate and William Thompson, gave evidence of having seen

115

Rotherham and/or Bess on the road around the time of the murder. It was they that sent Charles Rotherham to the gallows. Whether he would have escaped that appointment without their evidence is doubtful. The forces of law and order would have stopped at nothing to ensure that the verdict demanded was exactly the one delivered. Let's consider what the two of them had to say in a little more detail.

William Thompson was a resident of Mansfield. On July the 7th he was returning from Nottingham on foot. As far as it is possible to establish, Thompson's sighting of Rotherham took place at around 6.34 that evening, prior to the murder. In court he testified that he was sure that the man he had seen was Rotherham. Though he did not know Bess, he also said that he saw a young woman and described her remarkably accurately as being *about seventeen years of age.* He later confirmed her to be the same girl dragged from the ditch on the Nottingham road. Rotherham, he said, at the time of the sighting, was ahead of Bess and had nothing in his hands. He saw no-one else on the road.

July the 7th in the year of 1817 became an eventful day in the life of William Thompson only with the dawning of July the 8th. Only then was anyone outside of the participants aware that a murder had occurred. For Thompson, Monday the 7th was just another day. On his journey home from Nottingham he saw nothing of any consequence, nothing to distinguish that day from any other. The obvious question is then *why did he remember Charles Rotherham?* How could he be so sure when he stood in the courtroom that the man before him in the dock was the very same man he had seen casually, almost three weeks previous, passing him in the road? William Thompson, it seems, was a truly remarkable man. I defy anyone to reproduce such a feat of memory with regard to a recent observation when *nothing has occurred that renders that observation at all memorable.* Try it. You probably have without knowing it. Have you been out for a stroll on a Sunday afternoon after too indulgent a lunch? Maybe you called in the pub for a quick drink on the way home? Perhaps you stopped off at the market for some fresh veg? If so, do you remember the man who passed you in the park with the dog? What about the bloke in the pub standing by the games machine? On the market the man next to you buying brussel sprouts as you were given your change? Or was it a woman? More importantly, would you be able to remember them two and a half weeks after these non-events?

If your reply to these questions is, as I imagine, no, then you are not in the same league as William Thompson. Let me test you further. The man with the dog, the stranger in the pub, the person beside you on the market stall - what were they holding? You don't recall? William Thompson did, and he was a weary man who had walked from Nottingham after a busy day and was almost certainly wondering what he was getting for tea that evening and looking forward to a smoke and maybe a jug of ale. Yet far from recalling Rotherham carrying something distinctive that caught his eye, William Thompson recalled with enviable clarity that Charles Rotherham, two and a half weeks earlier, was carrying *nothing*. His abilities were, you must concede, quite uncanny.

I have no wish to decry William Thompson. He isn't, after all, around to answer any of my questions. However, by putting yourself in his position, I am not doubting his evidence, but rather, given similar circumstances, asking what credibility you would give your own?

Thomas Highgate almost emulates Thompson's expertise but in his evidence there is one fatal flaw.

117

Highgate, too, was in all probability a Mansfield man. He said he passed Charles Rotherham around seven o'clock, very soon after the murder. Highgate, too, identified Rotherham with the same certainty as Thompson. This is understandable, for Highgate had a better reason for remembering Rotherham for, by the time he saw him he *was* carrying something. He had, he said, *a bundle is his left hand and an umbrella in his right.* Good reason, no doubt, to look twice at so rough an individual. But why did he describe the contents of his left hand as a bundle? Did he not see the shoes allegedly taken from the body? He saw and identified the umbrella. Were the shoes concealed? Had Rotherham stuffed them in his *own* bag? But what bag? The Rotherham of minutes earlier was confidently described by William Thompson as being *empty-handed*. Were the shoes then wrapped in something else taken from Bess? We are not told that anything else was missing. Both bonnet and shawl were accounted for. Both were found near the scene. Is it not likely that Rotherham was indeed carrying a bundle? A bundle of his own possessions? Is it not likely, destitute as even he was supposed to be, that he would have something of his own with him? In fact he *was* carrying something. There is evidence that covers this.

Mary Pettinger at the Three Crowns pub where Rotherham stayed the night in Red Hill told the court that when he arrived he was carrying shoes, an umbrella *and* a bundle. A bundle which, it appears, escaped the otherwise hawk eyes of William Thompson.

But what is this fatal flaw in Highgate's evidence? In his attention to detail he missed one thing. Something which, were he to have spotted it, would surely have led to the earlier apprehension of Charles Rotherham, violent murderer. The obvious clue that seems to have escaped the attention of every single witness. *There was no blood.*

Descriptions of the crime in the press were nothing if not graphic. Bess' head had been caved in. Her brains protruded from her skull. One eye was knocked from its socket and dangled on her cheek. The hedgestake produced in court with such a flourish was caked with blood such that its appearance *struck feelings of horror into the court* three weeks afterwards.

Now I have never battered anyone's head to a pulp despite frequent temptation, nor have I ever searched a fresh body in a frenzy of sexual or monetary frenzy. I dare say that if I had I would surely bear the clear evidence of my deed. Never mind meticulous searches for DNA traces, I'd likely be covered in blood. The violence done to Bessie Sheppard was real, not the sanitised bang-you're-dead killing of pre-watershed TV. Can we really then be expected to believe that Rotherham, after so brutal a slaying, was not covered in the blood and the brain of his victim? An observation surely any potential witness would recall, would he not, and relish telling the court? Rotherham had had no time to clean up before passing Highgate.

Taking Highgate's evidence along with Thompson's, a disturbing pattern emerges. Thompson saw Rotherham *and remembered him to be empty-handed.* Highgate saw him and *remembered him to be carrying an umbrella and a bundle.* Each was positioned, miraculously, either side of the murder both geographically and chronologically. No-one else was seen by the pair on the road. How neatly the evidence fits the sequence of events Benjamin Barnes tells us occurred. How attentive the witnesses were to what Rotherham was or was not carrying, yet how Highgate missed the very thing that could have resulted in Rotherham's early arrest. Could it be that Messrs. Thompson and Highgate were so assured in their memories of that otherwise uneventful day because they had been schooled by Ben Barnes? How else can we account for the testimony

119

of Thompson where, in passing, he described the girl he only knew later to be Bess as being about seventeen? Such an uncannily accurate observation, I suggest, indicates knowledge gained after the murder, not surmised before.

On July the 8th, both of our prime witnesses had learned that the previous day had been more eventful than they had hitherto believed. Mansfield was alive with salacious gossip about the girl in the ditch. Thompson had been at the scene and identified her as the girl he had passed the day before. Very soon word would have arrived of a man having been arrested in Loughborough for the murder. Curiosity was aroused when they heard he was to be brought to Sutton-in-Ashfield, just up the road, to the Coroner's Court. Just as today crowds will lay siege to a courthouse to get a glimpse of a murderer, so in 1817 the desire for vicarious thrills would have drawn them to view Charles Rotherham. Rotherham sought - according to Barnes - to oblige them. At the inquest he submitted to the blood lust of the mob, insisting, so we are told, that he be paraded before them. It is not difficult to imagine that within that mob that gathered outside the Blue Bell would have been both Thomas Highgate and William Thompson. They would be more eager than most to once more glimpse the killer that they assumed had passed them on the road. There, in the square outside the inn, seeing the face of the man accused of murder, how could they forget him? It was, I suggest, *that* day, July the 8th, that was memorable in the minds of Thompson and Highgate. For it was that day, not the previous, when they had become familiar enough with the face of Charles Rotherham to be able to stand up in court and say, yes, that was him. How convenient that Rotherham had shown contrition to Barnes and had insisted he be paraded before the mob. But did he? We have only Ben Barnes' word for this. Remember, Rotherham never spoke except through Barnes. Is it beyond the realms of possibility that the whole show was staged by Barnes solely to ensure

120

that Rotherham's identification later in court was positive? How easy to transform a vague recollection, with careful tuition, into a certainty.

***

Let's go on to consider the evidence of William Ball, Robert Cheadle, Mary Pettinger and Ann Lewis. Here we face an altogether more thorny problem. All of these witnesses had ample time to get a good look at the man called Charles Rotherham. All but Ball gave evidence of him having either shoes, an umbrella, a bundle, or any permutation of the three at the time of their encounter with him. It would be difficult to challenge their identifications as being other than precise.

William Ball was an ex-soldier and probably shared some of the hardships of life with Rotherham upon discharge. He had served with the 9th Infantry and had, like as not, seen action in the Peninsular Wars. The Journal describes him as an acquaintance of Rotherham whom he accidentally met. The review makes no mention of this. It seems an unlikely coincidence that the men would know one another. They went to The Hutt together where Ball stated he spent fifteen minutes in Rotherham's company - a somewhat brief time for old comrades. They must have met around 7.15, twenty minutes or so after Bess' murder. They would, no doubt, have discussed the war and the hell of coming back home and trying to fit back into the community. Rotherham certainly told Ball that his wife had left him. This much Ball told the court.

What is extraordinary about the meeting, a meeting I repeat just twenty minutes after the slaying of Bess, is that nowhere in Ball's testimony does he mention Rotherham's appearance. Was he asked? There is no word of shoes, no mention of an umbrella (surely an odd item of note between ex-soldiers) nor of a *bundle*. Nor did he see blood. Why did

Ball, the very first person to have close contact with Rotherham so soon after the alleged crime had been committed, make no mention of the items stolen (so clear to Thomas Highgate) nor of the blood on his clothing? Had he not savoured the prospect of describing in court the signs which would later tie Rotherham to the bloody deed? I doubt it could have been that Rotherham had deposited his coat and booty with the hat check girl. So why? I would not challenge the fact that Ball did indeed meet Rotherham, but why did he see no blood? Perhaps the answer is *because there was none.* By that I do not imply the crime was bloodless - it patently was not - what I mean is that there was no blood to be seen upon the person of Charles Rotherham for the simple reason that he may not have been the killer of Elizabeth Sheppard.

Put yourself in Rotherham's position. At 6.52pm or thereabouts, you murder a young girl, perhaps as the result of an attempted rape. Maybe you hoped to find cash for more beer. Whatever the motive, you take a heavy hedgestake and beat her to death. You then toss the stake, dripping with her blood and brain tissue, into the ditch. You could not, you decide, just leave her there on the road, so you drag her over to the ditch that runs alongside the road and hope the body will not be found for a while. From the body you take the shoes and umbrella to sell later. You have very little time for this. What would your mental state be? Anything, I suggest, but calm and rational. You would, I suspect, be trembling with fear, suddenly rendered sober by the horrifying events of the last few minutes. You walk on. You see a stranger approaching you. Thomas Highgate. You do not learn his name until you're in court. In your hands are the spoils of your deed. You're in a state of acute anxiety. Had you hidden the body well enough? You could have made a better job given more time. Will it be discovered? Were there any signs of the scuffle on the road? You can't remember. Blood even? You didn't notice. Would there be enough to make the man stop and look around? There was enough to suggest this to John Womley next day and make him investigate.

Taking into account the probable mental state of a guilty Charles Rotherham a man fleeing the site of a recent killing, I suggest the very last thing he would contemplate is stopping off for a drink with William Ball. Even less likely would he be to *pass* The Hutt, as the evidence suggests, then *double back* toward the scene of the crime. Under such circumstances his first concern would be to get away, as far and as quickly as possible, from the immediate area. That Rotherham did not do this must cast doubt upon his guilt.

If Rotherham's behaviour is inconsistent with that of a murderer, with someone who has undergone the kind of trauma that made escape paramount, is it possible that he could have simply found the shoes and umbrella by the roadside, left by a killer too scared to spend adequate time covering his deed? Could he have come across them quite by chance, unaware they were the spoils of murder, and just take them on the off-chance he might make a couple of shillings? Maybe he was curious as to the origin of his windfall. Maybe he looked round. Perhaps he never even saw the body. He was drunk, maybe too drunk? But how could he have missed the body if he had looked round? Womley, in evidence, indicates that following the discovery of the button and the ball of cloth in the early hours of the 8th, he looked further. Womley left home at 6.15am. He lived in Mansfield, not an hour's walk from the murder site, yet it was not, he said, until *9.30am* that he found the body.

There is no explanation given for this delay, but what is apparent is that, on first looking, he too did not see Bess. Did he look again later? His evidence doesn't imply this. What other explanation could there be for such a delay? If Womley, fresh from his bed, was unable to locate Bess immediately, what chance a drunken Rotherham if the scenario I suggest was correct?

Perhaps then, without clear signs that violence was the reason for his good fortune, Rotherham felt able to take the shoes and umbrella and continue on his journey. He could pass Highgate without fear of blood being seen upon him. There was none. He could invite William Ball back to The Hutt for a drink because it was toward the scene of a crime of which he perhaps had no knowledge. In these circumstances Charles Rotherham was without fear for his life; there was no reason for him to run.

This version of events, taken in conjunction with the hatred of ex-soldiers, the eagerness of the police to prove themselves and the inadequacy of the judicial system, becomes less and less unlikely the more it is considered. One consequence of it, if it is true, is that less criticism need be directed at the evidence of subsequent witnesses, Cheadle and Pettinger at the Three Crowns and Ann Lewis at the Rancliffe Arms. All they testified to was Rotherham's possession of articles that had once been on the person of Bessie Sheppard. Taken in conjunction with the evidence of Thompson and Highgate, such information carried a certain weight. In isolation it proves nothing with regard to the crime for which Rotherham was tried. When doubt is cast upon the word of the two main witnesses, the cast iron case against Charles Rotherham begins to appear much less substantial.

William Ball's evidence, viewed objectively, actually says nothing other than Rotherham was around at the time. Indeed, it is what he does *not* say that renders Ball, far from being a rock for the prosecution, rather more a witness for the defence. Ball makes no mention of the shoes or umbrella. How could he have overlooked them, these objects recalled with such clarity by Thompson and Highgate both for their presence and their absence? How, after a significant period of time with Rotherham, could he have failed to notice blood on his person?

The only thing the court has, amid this veritable carnival of witnesses, is the confession of Charles Rotherham. A confession that issued, not from his own lips on such occasions as they could have been heard, but as hearsay from those of his supremely efficient captor, Benjamin Barnes. It is to him and the arrest we will now turn.

**

The Nottingham Journal in its report of the murder trial said,

"....the crime was marked with this peculiar feature, that the prisoner had received no provocation, nor could he assign any other motive for his inhuman conduct, than a sudden and fell desire, which took possession of his mind, to destroy the girl."

Rotherham had, we are told, admitted the killing of Bess, but had denied there having been any motive for the crime. He had had no compulsion to rape her, indeed, his vehement and consistent denial of this went unchallenged. He had no intention of robbing her for he had, according to Barnes, six shillings in his pocket at the time of the murder. In terms of worth in 2014 this would equate to around £20 sterling. The crime was motiveless.

The tacit acceptance on the part of the court of this irrationality sits uncomfortably with the facts. Quite why the authorities and the press puzzled so over the crime being motiveless is difficult to understand, when theft *had* so clearly taken place and when there were, from the state of Bess' clothing, strong indications of a sexual aspect to the crime. Far from being perplexed by an absence of motive, they were all but overwhelmed by their abundance. This oversight may seem trivial, but the proliferation of oversights on the part of the prosecution was beginning to indicate a very sloppy approach to the whole enquiry.

Let's look at the events of Tuesday, July the 8th.

The body was found at 9.30am by John Womley, the quarryman. The man and woman who passed by in the gig and who took the news to Nottingham could not have learned of the murder until after this time, possibly much later. The journey from the murder site to Nottingham - twenty-five minutes by car today - cannot have taken less than an hour by one-horsed carriage in 1817. The police in Nottingham could therefore not have learned of the murder until around 10.30am at the absolute earliest, and what they learned must even then have been minimal. Simply that a girl had been found in the ditch just outside Mansfield, battered to death. The infant constabulary, anxious to prove its worth, mobilised its forces. Ben Barnes was despatched on horseback to investigate. He could not have reached the scene before 11.30 at the earliest and again the probability is that it would have to be much, much later. Preliminary enquiries would have been instigated before Barnes arrival, but it seems unlikely that by the time he got there the victim could have been positively identified. Coming from Papplewick, she was not a local girl and her face and head were badly disfigured. We know from court evidence that Sarah Clay, the girl who gave so accurate a time for Bess leaving Mansfield, saw the body, but this could hardly have been until it had been removed from the ditch at 2.00pm.

So what could Barnes discover? More importantly, what time did he have available in which to make his enquiries, bearing in mind that, as a result of them, he had to get to Loughborough in order to arrest Rotherham *later that very afternoon?*

Events surrounding the time immediately following the discovery of the body are vague. Little is known outside of

126

the fact that Womley alerted lawyer Walkden and Colonel Need, two of the more influential men in Mansfield. The surgeon, John Batchelor, of Sutton-in-Ashfield, was fetched to examine the body, as was Richard Jepson, the Sutton parish constable. We know little else. We must again return to the problem of time in the story of the murder. Remarkably, the interviewing of witnesses, who had first to be identified and then located, the removal and identification of the body, all these time consuming necessities inhibited Benjamin Barnes not one whit. Within a few hours of viewing the body we know that he returned to Red Hill and called at the Three Crowns where Mary Pettinger gave him one of the shoes left by Rotherham. From there he continued on to the city itself where further unrecorded enquiries caused him to conclude that the very man he wanted, this Charles Rotherham, was heading toward the village of Bunny. Accompanied by Officer Linneker now, Barnes visited the Rancliffe Arms in Bunny where Ann Lewis, the proprietor, described the same man and told him that he had sold her an umbrella. Continuing southwards they arrested Charles Rotherham that very afternoon for the murder of a girl whose name they likely still did not know.

Ben Barnes was an exceedingly busy man. In that one day he must have covered, on horseback, some fifty miles prior to the arrest of Rotherham. One cannot but marvel at his stamina and stand in awe when faced with the power of his penetrating intuition. What, for instance, was it that he learned at the murder site that convinced him that his quarry had gone on to Nottingham and that no other line of enquiry was necessary. Remember, by the time he commits to returning to Nottingham in pursuit of the felon, neither Thompson or Highgate had probably been found to indicate that Nottingham was the direction in which he should go. Why was he so certain that the murderer had not gone to Blidworth or Kirkby or even into Mansfield itself? All these options were open at the Toll Bar. Was it sheer luck on Barnes' part, or did someone direct him?

We know that William Thompson saw the body and was able, using his formidable powers and despite Bess' features being *battered beyond recognition*, to identify the victim as the very stranger he had passed the day before. Whether Thompson saw the body in situ or viewed it after it had been transported to the Unicorn in Sutton for the post-mortem, is not clear. But it does seem unlikely he would have attended at the roadside. Why would he have felt the need? Assuming he had even heard of the killing that quickly, why would he associate it with the strangers he had passed the day before on the road? Monday the 7th of July was, for him, uneventful. What's more, on the face of it, there was no reason to even presume that the murder had been committed on the Monday. The body could have been in the ditch on the Sunday, could it not?

But let's assume that because of some great curiosity, both Thompson and Highgate were somehow drawn to that roadside on the morning of the 8th. What information could they have given Barnes? No more than the fact that between six-thirty and seven the previous evening they had seen a stranger on the road. Could this alone have been enough to despatch Barnes on his mission? The Nottingham road of the 7th of July was not exactly bereft of pedestrian traffic, strange or otherwise. Aside from Bess and Rotherham themselves there were at least three other travellers; Thompson, Highgate and William Ball. Travellers on that road were not uncommon. Mansfield was a coaching centre through which many strangers passed en route north and south. The presence of a stranger on the road would not seem to be a matter of any great significance.

But whatever happened that morning at the scene of Bess' murder, it was sufficient to convince Ben Barnes that it was the work of a stranger. An itinerant. One thing he could deduce from the condition of Bess' feet, was that she had been wearing shoes at the time she died. With no shoes found near the body it would seem likely that the killer had stolen them. It would also be logical for him to call at The Hutt, just along the road. There, no doubt, he would learn of an ex-soldier who had been drinking there the previous early evening. Was the mere mention of an ex-soldier enough to spur Barnes on? Were they not all unreliable bastards hardened to the casual taking of life? But why go after Rotherham alone? Hadn't there been *two* soldiers in The Hutt that Monday? Rotherham *and* Ball? Had not Ball, too, been in the right place at the right time? Wasn't Ball a stranger? Ball had been heading for Mansfield. Mansfield was nearer than Nottingham. Why head for Nottingham on what might be a wild goose chase when enquiries in Mansfield itself might have equally resulted in catching the killer? For what reason was William Ball apparently never considered as a suspect?

I believe something happened in the hours immediately following the discovery of the body. Something that convinced Ben Barnes he had best conduct his search for Bess' killer anywhere but in Mansfield itself. I believe someone was present at the murder site who, for reasons best known to themselves, saw to it that Barnes sought the murderer away from Mansfield. Someone who directed the police officer to pursue Rotherham to the exclusion of any other suspect. Someone who may well have even been in a position to supply the officer with the name of the vagrant only vaguely recalled by the passers-by of the previous evening. But more of that later.

After the most superficial of enquiries and with the encouragement of this unknown adviser, Barnes left for Nottingham, hopefully hot on the trail of the killer. Imagine his excitement on learning at the Three Crowns that his quarry had stayed the night and had left behind an

129

incriminating pair of girl's shoes. Whatever doubts he might have been harbouring were, with this information, completely dispelled. Thereafter he was single-minded. The vagrant from Sheffield was his man.

Rotherham thereafter stood no chance, Barnes simply had to find him. He pursued him assiduously through Nottingham and on southwards. Unnecessary as seemed the need for further proof, his conviction that Rotherham was his man could only have increased when he met Ann Lewis at the Rancliffe Arms and obtained corroborative details of the same man. Barnes made his remarkable arrest on the bridge, just north of Loughborough, on the afternoon of Tuesday the 8th of July. Bess had not been dead twenty-four hours.

The pursuit and capture of Rotherham demonstrated, if nothing else, remarkable determination on the part of Ben Barnes - and not a little luck. Indeed, were we still to pursue the search for Lord Lucan, there would be no better person to call than Ben Barnes. With the later confirmation that the girl had been seen to be carrying an umbrella, all doubt as to the guilt of his captive must have vanished. Charles Rotherham *was* the murderer.

But Ben Barnes made one fatal assumption. Fatal, that is, for Charles Rotherham. In his haste to catch the murderer, he assumed possession of the articles from the crime scene constituted irrevocable proof that whoever possessed them had to be the killer. Prejudice and ignorance played a major distorting role. Rotherham, both an ex-soldier and a vagrant, was also surely a killer. Of that there was no doubt. But Barnes knew such a conclusion was not fully supported by the facts. He needed something else. That something was not long in being furnished.

When he was arrested, Charles Rotherham had nothing in his possession to link him with the murder of Bessie

Sheppard directly. Unless Barnes had been supplied with his name by an informant he had nothing even to indicate that the man staring into the stream just outside Loughborough was the man described by the witnesses. Nothing, that is, until he noticed spots of blood on Rotherham's collar and neckerchief. Spots of blood that had gone unnoticed by everyone else who had come into contact with Rotherham. Spots of blood which would, by the very words used by Barnes to describe them in court, seem inconsistent with what one would have expected to find on the person of someone guilty of so bloody a crime.

Blood from the body was the very thing Barnes needed to make the case against Rotherham airtight. But what if Barnes only saw on Rotherham precisely what all the other witnesses had seen? Nothing. What could he do? This was the murderer, wasn't it? Barnes logic put that beyond doubt. Barnes, I suggest, did what so many law enforcement officers have since seen fit to do to secure a conviction they saw to be in the public interest. He hardened up the evidence by tampering. A quiet word in the ears of Thompson and Highgate would ensure the crystal clarity of their recall. The supposed blood on Rotherham would have, anyway, faded by the time of the trial, making its absence invite no unwanted questions. A confession, he had no doubt, could be made forthcoming. Benjamin Barnes had nothing to lose - and everything to gain.

***

It need hardly be repeated that the early years of the nineteenth century were not amongst the best in which to be arrested in England, least of all for murder. With the suspension of Habeas Corpus, under which detention of an individual had to have at least tenuous links with the commission of a crime, there were no longer restrictions on a person's arrest. Coupling the universal vilification of vagrant and ex-serviceman (doubly harsh where the two

131

categories are combined) with a virgin police force anxious to make its mark, one can easily imagine the treatment meted out to such accused. Prospects for Charles Rotherham were bleak indeed. Both vagrant, an ex-soldier and a drunkard to boot, witnessed to have been near the scene of a brutal murder and suspected of having been in possession of various articles taken from the deceased, he had little, if anything, going for him. Barnes had in custody the man he *knew* was guilty. That Rotherham had, at the time of arrest, been likely to deny his guilt was only to be expected. They all did. With two hundred or more capital offences on the statute it was a natural response to deny anything and everything. For Charles Rotherham it could have been natural under a number of different sets of circumstances.

The reflex denial, I'll set aside. That's not the purpose of this book. There are, however, three other possible scenarios in which a denial might have been forthcoming and which warrant examination. Firstly, that he did in fact kill her but was too drunk at the time to remember it. Secondly, that he simply did not do it and had no knowledge of either the dead girl or the items stolen from her. Lastly, that he did not kill Bess but that he *did* steal her belongings either directly from the body - in which case he knew of the crime - or from nearby and oblivious to the presence of the body in the ditch.

The first option is unsatisfactory for several reasons, but in the absence of a full confession for the police to work with it would suffice and Rotherham would still hang. However, to consider it as a real possibility requires the acceptance of the evidence of Thompson, Highgate and Ball, riddled as it was with both fantastic feats of memory and startling oversights, as being accurate in every respect. The murder would have had to be virtually bloodless. We would have to be prepared to accept that none of the witnesses noticed, or at least failed to remark upon,

Rotherham's probable drunken state. We would have to be content not to question how a man in such a condition might be capable of making the journey he did at the speed he did, yet be utterly devoid of any memory of the crime. Under such a chain of events, one in which we would expect a total denial, could we nevertheless ignore our doubts and hand the man over to the hangman? I think not.

What then of the possibility that Rotherham neither killed Bess, nor did he steal her belongings? We would, were we to believe such an option, have to seriously doubt every single subsequent identification and any of the evidence given after William Ball. This includes the separate testimonies of Pettinger and Lewis. While perfectly possible to question each identification of Rotherham in isolation, taken together they become significant and substantial. Add to that the fact that both women had close dealings with him, thus giving them good reason to remember him. We must, I believe, accept their evidence as being accurate and of a reliability much higher than that of Thompson and Highgate.

All that remains for consideration is the final option in which Rotherham took the shoes and umbrella but did not commit murder. Did he take them from the body directly or did he pick them up by the side of the road, oblivious to the body in the ditch, and before anyone else had the time to pass by?

The same argument used earlier must again be applicable here. Had Rotherham *seen* the body and knowingly stolen from it, then his reactions after the event must surely, I suggest, have been similar, if not identical to, those he would have had were he the murderer. He would have had, would he not, the same overwhelming desire to make himself scarce. He knew that were he found in the immediate vicinity of the body he would certainly be arrested for the murder. He would, likewise, have been in no

133

mental state to enjoy the company of William Ball in The Hutt.

So, we're left with the option of Rotherham simply finding the shoes and umbrella. Though in some sort of control of his faculties, he was still the worse for drink and could well have overlooked the presence of a body in the ditch, much as John Womley initially did the following morning. But Ben Barnes would never accept this. It was just not in his interests to entertain such a proposition, not even if Linneker - the officer strangely not called to give evidence to the court - perhaps found it not totally unconvincing. Denial of the murder was unthinkable, if expected. There existed in those days, we must remember, no accepted protocol governing the handling of suspects. The press, from the outset, were ranged against Rotherham, setting him centre stage as the clear culprit. Where did they get their information. Then, as now, from the police. From Ben Barnes. How did they learn of his confessions prior to the court case? From Barnes, the only soul on earth, it seemed, privy to Rotherham's conscience A fair trial seemed unlikely.

Consider the circumstances surrounding the confession detailed to the court but conveniently denied them the privilege of hearing first hand. I can substantiate not one iota of what follows, yet I suggest the stretch of the imagination required is not excessively taxing. I find it entirely possible that Rotherham was put under some sort of duress to obtain the confession. It still happens. The methods may be more sophisticated and subtle and there are increasing forensic considerations to render such evidence insufficient by itself, but it still happens. The fervour of the infant force in Regency England together with their lack of accountability did little, I suggest, to dull the appetite for results.

134

Thereafter Rotherham says nothing except for that which is reported to us by Benjamin Barnes. He became, it seems, totally co-operative, explaining down to the last detail his crime. He generously (and it has to be said, somewhat needlessly) showed Barnes *on the return trip from the Inquest in Sutton to the Nottingham Gaol* precisely where he obtained the hedgestake with which he killed Bess. But why didn't they go there *on the way* to the Inquest, where such information might have been useful? The site of the murder is not located on the direct route between Nottingham to Sutton. For Barnes to discover this only after the Inquest, merely served to embellish his testimony and underline his thoroughness at the trial.

But, did all this happen? Was Charles Rotherham subjected to maltreatment to obtain his confession? There are two small observations which, though they may fall well short of proof, do go some way to support the contention that Rotherham's confession might not have been wholly voluntary. When Ben Barnes was in the witness box he was specifically asked by Sergeant Vaughan, the police officer conducting the prosecution (and no doubt a colleague of Barnes) whether *any threats or promises had been held out to Rotherham to induce him to confess.* Notwithstanding the difficulty I have imagining quite what *promises* might be made, I find it curious that the question was asked at all. Were the crowds gathered in the courtroom only too familiar with police methods to make such a disclaimer necessary? Pressure put on a suspect in one form and another was routine, wasn't it? Additionally, the confessions of Rotherham seem to have been, at times, somewhat contradictory. In one version of the confession related by Barnes to the court, Rotherham is said to have *come up behind the girl.* In another, given by the same officer, he is said to have told the police that it happened *when she came up to him.* This breakdown in consistency within so short a period of time leads me to suspect that Barnes hadn't fully

135

made his mind up quite what he wanted to say Rotherham had told him had happened that evening. The confessions of Charles Rotherham, far from sounding convincing, begin to take upon themselves the tone of a tired and beaten man, with little left to survive for, willing to agree to any suggestions regarding events that evening simply to be left in peace.

Barnes could easily have manipulated the evidence, pressured Rotherham, schooled the witnesses and then, being not quite the fixer he imagined himself to be, wasn't able to adequately remember who he'd decided did what to whom and when.

The authorities didn't have to sustain this deceit for long. By Monday the 28th of July, three weeks to the day after the murder and just three days after the end of the trial, Charles Rotherham went to the gallows.

Aside from challenging the case against Rotherham in the fairest way I believed I could, there were other concerns to which I had to turn my attention. Concerns which, while not serving to exonerate the dead man, certainly did nothing to underline his guilt. I looked to the town of Mansfield itself and the further events that were reported in the press. Events which deepened the mystery surrounding the name of Elizabeth Sheppard.

***

From the murder of Bess through to the marriage of Hetty I had advanced the Sheppard bloodline by just seventy short years. Though the work had been painstaking it had been worthwhile. I now sensed I was within striking distance of a living survivor. I make no pretence that my approach to genealogy had been through the seat-of-the-pants, pick it up while you go along school of historical research. Outside of an awareness of the existence of

136

Somerset House and a reluctance to pay for what had been hitherto free, I was unsure as to how I could make any further progress. There was a problem on the near horizon. A marathon runner hits the wall at twenty-two miles. I knew mine awaited me, for, just after the turn of the century the access to parish records expired. I faced what I could only see as documentary exhaustion and knew that, were Hetty and William Dickinson not obliging enough to produce another child before the turn of the century, the problems that would follow would be both enormous and potentially costly.

Let me briefly elaborate. During the latter years of my research I had tried to trace the army and apprenticeship records of Charles Rotherham held in the Public Record Office at Kew. I employed a private researcher, a PhD., whose name I obtained from the documents supplied by the PRO. At a cost of £15 an hour (pricey back then) he made the search. It culminated in a substantial bill just prior to Christmas. My first wife and I had two children and no great income. And, for my money - and this is not the doctor's fault - I got precisely nothing. The records may have been there, probably *were* there, concealed within a vast mountain of documentation and I just couldn't afford to keep looking for them.

Hetty and William, I'm pleased to say, did not fail me. On April 13th 1889 they had a daughter. Elizabeth again, whom they had baptized on July the 3rd of that year. Their address was recorded as 48, Newgate Lane, Mansfield. I drove there and began excitedly to check the door numbers. Where number 48 should have been stood just the remains of a worn front step and a small, stone boundary wall. Where the room had been in which the infant Elizabeth would have slept in her cot beside the coal fire slumped a derelict Reliant Robin.

137

Had Elizabeth Dickinson survived into her seventieth year, she would have carried the line from Bess tantalisingly close to the present. She would have died when I was twelve and been a contemporary of my grandmother. But what became of her I have no idea. The lack of records made of the narrow gap between her and the present day a yawning chasm.

I embarked upon a futile round of door to door enquiries in the area of the old Dickinson home in the vain hope that someone behind one of the doors would remember them. I shuttled between pensioner's bungalows and old folk's homes in the pursuit of.....well, what? Were I, unlikely as it might seem, to come across someone who recalled the family, what chance was there of them knowing where they now lived or what became of them? Elizabeth Dickinson, by the time she had children of her own, would have a different name, herself having married.

I knew what my new strategy would have to be - I was just hoping I could avoid it. In order to move *down* the Dickinson line, I would first have to reverse my direction and move back *up* it from today. I would need to collect as many names together as I could and go public. It was a long shot, but it was all I had and it had the great virtue of being cheaper than the alternatives. Hours spent hunched over micro-film furnished me with a list of names and dates for the Dickinson clan that I hoped would jog the memory of someone, somewhere. Armed with pre-typed letters, envelopes, stamps and reply envelopes I repaired to the local pub during lunch breaks where I wrote to every Dickinson in the phone book. Draining the dregs of my last pint, I rose, crossed my fingers and went outside to post the letters, feeling lost and not a little stupid.

***

138

By this time my first marriage had ended and I had remarried. I'd been upstairs all evening writing and had totally forgotten to eat. At around eight-thirty my stomach cramps reminded me that food wasn't such a bad idea, so I went downstairs to make a sandwich. The phone rang while I was in the kitchen. Chris, my second wife, answered it. I assumed, as usual, it would be her parents at this time of day.

"It's a Mr Dickinson," she said, poking her head round the kitchen door.

It had been at least two weeks since I had sent out all my mail shots and I had all but given up hope of any replies of significance. I took the phone.

The voice on the other end of the line was deep and authoritative. The caller was, he explained. responding to the letter he had received and apologised for not having rung sooner as he had been away. He assumed the murder I had obliquely referred to was the only local one he had heard of, that of Bessie Sheppard. I confirmed his assumption and, in my excitement, forget much of the next few minutes of conversation. Suffice it to say, the names in the letter had meant something to him. I was stunned. I had waited twenty years for this moment. Barry Dickinson, my caller, had no way of knowing how important it was to me. His voice cast a line into the past. He invited me round for coffee on the evening of Wednesday the 1st of September.

***

I arrived at the end of the street where Barry Dickinson lived a little before eight in the evening, both excited and not a little nervous. This could be a massive step forward in my search, perhaps the end of my story, but it could also be, had I made some awful cock-up along the way, a complete fiasco. What if some chance remark were to cast doubt on

139

all my years of investigation? It was unlikely, I consoled myself; hadn't I checked and re-checked everything a thousand times? Well yes, but that thousand and first look....?

I glanced at my watch. It was eight. I rolled the car forward and stopped outside the door. Barry Dickinson was, as I had anticipated he would be, an organised, articulate man. He had clearly prepared for my visit if the spiral bound notebook on the coffee table in front of him was anything to go by. It would be understandable, perhaps, were I to confess to having scanned his face for some echo of the Sheppard characteristics, but to be honest, such thoughts were far from my mind.

To my delight Barry's father was present too. A lovely old gentleman of eighty-eight, William Henry Dickinson possessed, as do many of his age, a remarkable memory for the past. He was able, for instance, to recite in order the names of the families that had lived on Newgate Lane some seventy or eighty years previous.

I experienced brief moments of what I hope were contained panic when we were unable to agree upon the door number of one of his ancestors, William Dickinson Junior. The door number I possessed just seemed to him too high for the location he recalled them having lived on the street. I was worried lest a rogue William Dickinson had emerged from the woodwork to pour cold water on my efforts. Then, to my relief, Barry's father remembered that Newgate Lane had, back in those days, a convolution of multiple alleyways and cul-de-sacs wound up in a serpentine arrangement. This concentration of stone cottages into so small an area could easily account for the paradoxically high door number I had recorded.

It was impossible, looking at Bill (and I call him this not through familiarity, but merely to distinguish him from the myriad William Dickinsons that populated my story) not to see him as a direct link with the past. Bill had *known* these people who hitherto had been to me just pieces in a jigsaw that spread thinly over a hundred and fifty years. He immediately breathed life into the past, made it real. What was for him a reminiscence was for me an adventure.

I spent an hour and a half there. There would be, I was sure, a thousand questions that occurred to me after I left. My notebook was a confusion of names and relationships, anecdotal remarks and indecipherable nonsense. It was to be a long night. I had to beat it into some sort of shape while it was still fresh in my mind. The problem was, while answering a host of questions, my ninety minutes with the Dickinsons had posed new, potentially unanswerable ones.

The bloodline from Elizabeth Sheppard that ran, via Hetty Sheppard, into the veins of the Dickinson children had, just prior to the outbreak of World War One, transferred to Barrow-in-Furness in Cumbria with the relocation of the family. Whilst that was bad enough, worse was still to come. Of the many children born to Hetty and William Dickinson, there were just two through whom I hoped I might fruitfully pursue my search. Neither were the two on which I had originally pinned my hopes. One , yet another Elizabeth, the other, a son, Harry. Elizabeth married a dubious character called Billy Molloy, who disappeared, the children of the union somehow winding up as orphans in Nazareth House Orphanage in Lancaster. Harry, whom I had decided had to be the eldest son of Hetty, was a much bigger problem. I had him, Bill assured me, in the wrong place on the family tree. Harry was not the *son* of William Dickinson Jnr but the *brother*, the son of William Dickinson Snr through his marriage to Martha. I could hardly argue with his assertion, much as I would have liked, for Harry was Bill's father.

The children left to pursue were both female, Nell and Hetty Jnr. Nell, however, only had daughters and her married name was unknown. The line of Hetty Jnr was even less promising. She married a Peruvian called Mendiola, a South American representative at the Barrow shipyards where her father worked, deployed there in the early years of the Great War. Had she remained in England the tracing of a Mendiola family would have proven little problem among the Smiths and Browns, but no, Hetty returned to Peru with her new husband. The needle once more slipped back into the haystack.

Bill told me that Hetty Jnr had two children of whose names he was aware - Frida and Anthony. Anthony Mendiola, when last heard of, worked for a Peruvian airline and was based at Lima, the country's capital. He would, by now, be in his fifties.

The night after the meeting with the Dickinsons seemed endless. Already exhausted from absorbing the new information, I then endeavoured to collate it, finally crawling into bed in the early hours and slipping into a troubled sleep, from which, four hours later, I abruptly emerged, my problems still infuriatingly intact.

***

The new dawn, however, brought new resolve. I would *not* be beaten by a small inconvenience like the Atlantic Ocean. I rang the Peruvian Embassy in London, half expecting a thick, Latin-American accent on the line. What I got was the rich, deep sonorous voice of a distinctly British baritone. I was advised to apply in writing for help to the Ambassador in Sloane Square, London. I rang the Barrow-in-Furness library for the name and address of their main local newspaper and to check if there were any Dickinsons in the phone book. There were. Thankfully these were the days before the ubiquitous mobile. At lunchtime, a quick sortie in my own local library revealed that neither me nor Bill Dickinson had been in error the previous evening. There *were* two Harry Dickinsons. One was, indeed, Bill's dad, aged ten on the 1891 census. The other was his cousin, the first born son of William Dickinson Jnr. I was off the hook.

By the evening, letters were on their way to the Peruvian Embassy in London and the local Barrow paper. I rang the Dickinsons with my news, to resolve a minor query and to promise them copies of some of the records I had unearthed in my research. Barry Dickinson's wife answered the phone. Bill, it seemed, had been round earlier and had brought a photograph of Hetty Sheppard.

"Pardon?" I said.

"A photo of Hetty," she repeated. "Would you like to fetch it?"

That night I slept like a baby.

***

The sepia tone print was small. No more than three inches by two. It had it seemed, at some time in its history, been hacked from a larger print.

The faces of four women stared at me. It was strange. In some way I had half expected their gaze to be accusing, as if they could resent my disturbing their pasts. But they were not. The women seemed to court the camera. So many old photographs capture just the severity of their subjects, but these women were not severe. Their eyes had a gentleness I had not expected. The fourth lady, the eldest of the group, was different. I worked it out. She was fifty-six when the photo was taken in the 1920s.

This fourth lady was Hetty Sheppard, the great niece of Bess and granddaughter of Bess' brother, Joseph. If in the features of Hetty Sheppard there was even the faintest echo

143

of Bess' face then I knew why I had been drawn to her. Hetty's face was warm, kind and gentle. Perhaps beguiling is the correct word, for at fifty-six this lady retained a depth of beauty that time so rarely leaves intact. There was not here the usual, and expected, pain of having just survived. Here was joy. If my search took me no further than Hetty Sheppard's face, then the trip had been worthwhile.

***

In the examination of the events surrounding the murder of Bessie Sheppard I have tried to redress the imbalance of history by giving back to Charles Rotherham a voice, albeit belatedly, in his defence. He forfeited his life in silence and such silence is unjust. I have tried to sow seeds of doubt where hitherto there have been none and, such success as has been achieved is for you, not I, to judge. If doubt does exist now in your mind, a new question has to be asked. If Charles Rotherham did not kill Elizabeth Sheppard, then *who did*?

When I first hesitantly posed that question years ago my immediate response was that it was just too late to find an answer. However, as my enquiries progressed, I came upon things that I could not satisfactorily explain away. But to search for the definitive killer of Bessie Sheppard among the ghosts of the past would be as fruitful as listening for whispers in a thunderstorm. All I can do is to tell you that the intrigue surrounding Bess did not end with the hanging of Charles Rotherham. It continued beyond. In considering these later events I want to edge perhaps closer to the truth and, before I conclude, put forward another interpretation of what may have happened in the July of 1817.

***

144

On the 3rd of October 1817, almost three months after the murder, the following item appeared in the Nottingham Review:

On Tuesday evening, a play and farce was performed at the Theatre, Mansfield, by a party of young gentlemen of that place, assisted by Messrs. Clarke and Pritchard, and the Misses Pierce and Hargrave, from the Nottingham company, for the benefit of the mother of Elizabeth Sheppard, who was murdered on the Forest of Sherwood in July last. The play selected for the occasion, was Mr C Kemble's entertaining comedy of "The Point of Honour" or "The Noble Deserter", after which a monody, written for the occasion by Mr James Woods, was recited, together with dancing and comic singing; to which was added the admired farce of "The Register Office" and the whole concluded with "God Save the King". The Theatre at an early hour was crowded to excess, and it was much regretted that its limited extent rendered it necessary to close the doors, and thereby cause great disappointment to many, who could not, however anxious, obtain admission, as no doubt the receipts of the house would have been nearly double the sum - the house calculated to hold £28 admitted on this occasion £32. With respect to the performers, it is just to observe that Mr Clarke, in "Chevalier de St. Fraue" was truly excellent, Mr Pritchard was a real Durimel, the ladies also displayed considerable talent; the Mansfield gentlemen Mr Ellis, Mr Bramwell, Mr Bogg, Messrs S and J Shearman, and Master Wood, all played their respective parts, in a style, that would have done credit to performers of a mature age. The band of the Harmonic Society, generously assisted on the occasion, and the whole was received with marked and decided applause.

My curiosity was aroused, not from any desire to learn where the author derived his quaint feel for punctuation, nor from my ignorance as to quite what a monody was (in fact, a

145

Greek style lament on death that is written in verse), but from the fact that the event took place at all. I was unsure what to make of it. Was it, as first seemed, out of a genuine desire to help Mary Sheppard? Certainly the £32 raised (£2000 plus by 2014 values) could be put to good use by her if, as seems now even more likely, there was no husband on the scene and with the death of Bessie they had lost their sole wage earner. That could well have been all there was to it. But then, I wondered, didn't Mansfield have its full share of needy inhabitants who could themselves benefit from such charity? Why extend their generosity to a family of strangers from Papplewick?

I searched through reams of newspapers for evidence of similar events being staged for the bereaved of Mansfield. I found nothing. So why do this for Elizabeth Sheppard and her surviving family? Was there some other motive for the inexplicable warmth offered this nobody that went beyond mere charity? My initial disquiet regarding the stone monument on the roadside returned. It had, it said, been erected by the *Gentlemen of Mansfield.* Why were these *Gentlemen of Mansfield* so moved by this young girl who, as far as I could tell, had led her life in total anonymity for all of her seventeen short years, seven miles away in a tiny village? A girl whose sole claim to fame was that of being a victim and who was ignored in local histories but for that fact? Was there more to Bessie Sheppard than met the eye, and were there people who preferred it that way?

I delved deeper into the papers, right through to 1819. On the 3rd of April of that year the following piece appeared in response to the erection of the stone:

Mary Sheppard begs to offer her most grateful thanks to the nobility and gentry etc. of the town of Mansfield and its vicinity, for the many favours and kind assistance she has received since the murder of her daughter, Eliz. Sheppard; and humbly trusts, that the almighty will reward them an

146

hundred-fold in this world, and that they may become the partakers of eternal happiness thereafter.

Mary Sheppard,

Papplewick, April 1st, 1819.

Inadequate though it was as a tribute to Bess, conceived seemingly more as a memorial to death and, significantly, to keeping the perpetrator of that death in the public eye, the stone moved Mary Sheppard sufficiently to make the above reply. She was quite specific in giving her thanks, not to the people of Mansfield, but to the cream of the town, *the nobility and gentry.*

Who were these men, these gentlemen, to whom Mary extended such fulsome thanks? Why was it they rallied round in the hour of need? Another search, it seemed, was called for. It led me to places I could never have expected, but which, on later reflection, were no real surprise at all.

***

The Swan Hotel in Mansfield was, in 1817, run by a woman called Stirrup. In October of that year she handed over responsibility for it to her son, Samuel Stirrup. The Swan was an important coaching inn, giving rest and refreshment to many travellers en route to and from London. Each Monday auctions were held there that attracted substantial numbers of both potential buyers and the simply curious. It lay but a stone's throw from the mill owned by Hancock and Wakefield in which the young Sarah Clay, the girl who saw Bess leave Mansfield and was able to give such a precise time for her departure, was employed. From both the mill and The Swan the clock on the steeple of St. Peter's church is visible.

In the book "The History of Mansfield and its Environs" (William Harrod 1801), the following is recorded:

147

At the Swan Inn is the coffee room, held by subscription of many of the noblemen and gentlemen of the county, and principal tradesmen of the town, who are chosen by ballot.

I had always assumed, both because of the area and because Sarah Clay worked in a mill, that Bess herself had sought similar employment. This assumption was without foundation and possible quite wrong. There were, after all, mills in Papplewick where she could have worked. That being the case, why come to Mansfield? Could the attraction of the auctions, held on Mondays, have drawn her to the Swan? The hustle, the bustle; would they not have been a magnet for a young girl? For a lively girl like Bess the town held much more excitement and much more opportunity. Had Sarah Clay seen her at the Swan she would have been ideally placed to note the time shown on the church clock. Could Bess have gone to the Swan for work? She had, after all, worn her new shoes and carried a smart umbrella. It seemed as likely a destination as the mills. Could the excitement around the activity of the auction have accounted for Bess losing track of time and leaving Mansfield late? Could this be why Sarah Clay noted the time so accurately?

And what of this Society based at the Swan. These *noblemen and gentlemen* who took new members only by ballot? Who were they?

***

Reluctant though I was to accept the possibility that these influential men, who restricted membership of their ranks to a hand-picked elite, could be Freemasons, they certainly sounded like them. If pressed I would be compelled to admit to considering them sad individuals and not a little infantile. In the late seventies and eighties of the last millennium a veritable tidal wave of books flooded the market blaming the Freemasons for everything from the assassination of the Pope, the Ripper killings and complicity in concealing the

148

Holy Grail. It became routine, on picking up the latest conspiratorial tome to reach the bookstands, to flip to the index for the chapter on Freemasonry. It was inevitably there.

The individuals who gathered in the Swan, I'm pleased to say, were not Freemasons and consequently that movement has nothing to fear from my enquiry.

Now the Oddfellows, they're another thing altogether.

***

On the genealogical front things had gone quiet. I received no replies from Barrow-in-Furness where I had placed letters in the local paper, nor had the Peruvian Embassy in London deigned to contact me. I tried several desperate ways to revitalise progress. I wrote to the British Embassy in Peru's capital, Lima, and to the only Peruvian that I had ever heard of, the late Michael Bentine of 'Goon Show' and 'It's a Square World' fame. He was unable to help, but, unlike the Embassy and despite his illness, he at least took the time to write to me on a couple of occasions, somewhat belatedly warning me not to let the affair become an obsession!

It was a Saturday morning at around eight o'clock. Chris and I had planned a lie in. I heard the post fall on the hall mat. Being already awake I went downstairs to make a pot of tea and pick up the mail. A brown envelope with an official franking was folded in half and lodged in the letter box. As I pulled it free a second, blue envelope fell out. The official looking letter was from Chris' trade union. The blue envelope, I noticed, had written at the foot of my address on the front the word *England.* Picking it up I saw it bore the marking *via aerea.*

My excitement grew and with it that old familiar dread. I had been disappointed so often. It would be official and

149

quite polite, but would doubtless inform me that they were unable to help. The *they* being the British Embassy.

"What's the post?" Chris called from the bedroom.

"Just a letter from your union," I replied, "and, er, something from Peru."

Whether it was my imagination or not, I swear that her ensuing silence was punctuated by a cautious intake of breath.

"Oh," she said, all but inaudibly.

I took the letter into the bathroom with me and perched on the lavatory seat. I proceeded to open it as carefully as I could, as if a rougher approach might affect what it contained. A single sheet of blue paper lay within bearing the ambassador's crest.

Embajada Britanica, Lima, it read. *6 May, 1994.*

Fear prevented me from reading the text immediately. Perhaps I could stave off the disappointment that was surely round the corner if I just allowed the words to drift from the page. Hands shaking, I read on:

Dear Mr Marshall,

We acknowledge and thank you for your letter recently arrived,

We are glad to inform you that we have made contact with Mr Anthony Mendiola Dickinson to whom we have sent a copy of your letter and he will write to you directly. Just in case, his address follows....

Wishing you success with your research and looking forward to hearing from you, sincerely yours,

Lia Montes de Oca.

150

Social Secretary to the Ambassador.

I was suddenly aware that I was shaking from head to foot, desperately trying to work out what was more appropriate, laughter or tears.

"They've found him," I said to Chris as I re-entered the bedroom.

Somewhat daunted by the sight of this madman she had married standing in front of her on the point of apoplexy, she sat back on the bed, twisting her hands in her lap and watching me until confident I was calm enough not to be a threat to life and limb. If Lia Montes de Oca had walked in, I'd have kissed her - or him. I read and re-read the letter countless times, putting it safely with my papers in my desk, only to return to it periodically through the day to make sure I hadn't been dreaming. Years of work had paid off. I'd found Bess' living family. I'd found her great, great, great nephew. It warranted two bottles of Rioja that night.

The Monday after the arrival of the Embassy letter, a second letter arrived, this time by recorded delivery and post-marked *Peru*. The letter from Tony Mendiola ran to ten pages,. spanned two days in the writing and was brimming with energy and excitement. By the end of page eight, the end of his first day's toil on the screed, he felt sufficiently comfortable to write;

"...since by this time you know so much about me and my family, I will just sign off simply as....Tony.

At first reading little of the content sank in. I felt, however, the warmth and sincerity within it. It was reassuring to discover that, in Tony Mendiola, I had found the very person I always hoped would lie at the end of the trail. Someone to whom I could safely hand Bess' memory secure in the knowledge that it would be cherished as she deserved. With Tony and his family the line was re-established. Bessie Sheppard would survive in the minds of folk in a continent beyond her imagination.

Anthony Mendiola Dickinson was born in 1941. He's six years my senior. He lives in Callao, Peru with his sister Frida, born in 1916. He has a son, Raphael, in Bakersfield, California and a sister Nancy in the same state. In addition, if my count is correct, he has, or had, at least nine more siblings. With each new reading of the letter Tony fired new life into those who up till now had been mere names.

Richard Sheppard, Joseph's son and Bess' nephew was, by all accounts, a bright lad, but one with a penchant for beer. His schoolmaster, a strict Quaker, would constantly chase the errant Dick from the pubs with cries of:

Dick Sheppard, I taught you many good things at school, but never to come to places like this!

Hetty Dickinson, the lady of such singular beauty in the photograph, was widowed in the late twenties when William died. She re-married a man called Wain who suffered from acute bronchitis and whose treatment for the condition involved swathing his chest in raw bacon wrapped over with flannel. Tony describes Hetty with great warmth. She was a fun loving woman who adored the movies but, being unable to read, had trouble with the sub-titles on the silent films. The talkies, when they arrived, were a godsend. She would go from cinema to cinema, never growing bored. In Hetty I detected some of the spirit I always thought of as living within Bess.

It was Hetty's daughter, Hetty junior, who married Manuel Torcuato Mendiola Cockburn, the man whose existence the previous September had seemed to signal the end of my search. They married in 1914. In 1916, Manuel, a student of engineering at Vickers Armstrong shipyard in Barrow, was called away to aid a Peruvian ship that had run

152

aground off the coast of Wales and from there returned to Peru without his wife and family. They followed on later in 1921 when they could afford the passage. Hetty junior, Tony's mother, died in childbirth in Peru in November 1946 aged just forty-nine. She had borne twelve children. Scrawled along the margin of the letter Tony had added,

I once heard say, in Dallas, Texas; keep your wife at home, barefoot and pregnant.

Senor Mendiola certainly seems to have heeded the advice. In May 1949 Manuel Mendiola married Hetty's sister, Winnie. It was she who raised Tony and lived with him till her death in 1984 at the age of eighty-two.

The detail was endless and fine - and I have saved the best till last. Early in the letter Tony mentioned Richard Sheppard who had endured so tragic a life losing virtually all his close kin within a cruelly short period of time. Tony had a photograph of him! I wrote back that night, sending as much information as I could about his family and pleading for pictures of himself and, particularly, of Richard. I promised myself then and there that I would keep in touch with Tony Mendiola. I owed him. Perhaps one day, I wondered, we might meet. I would dearly love to shake the man by the hand.

Richard Sheppard.

The resourceful nephew of Bess, son of

her brother Joseph, and the man

who gave me the link to today.

The Dickinson ladies. Hetty, daughter of Richard Sheppard, is at the back dressed all in black.

Tony Mendiola with his sister, Frida, in Peru.

The family who now have custody of the memory

of Bessie Sheppard.

The Sheppard Family Tree

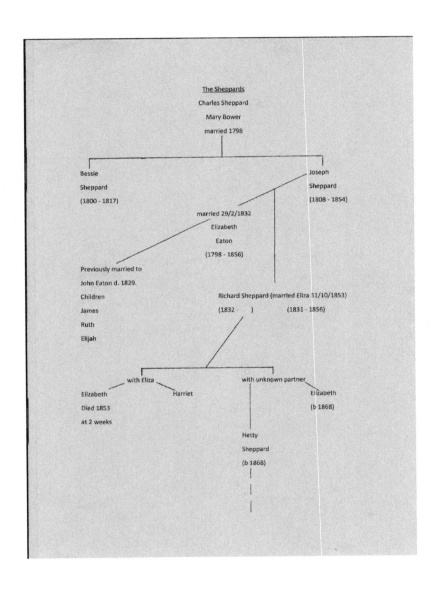

The Dickinson Family Tree

157

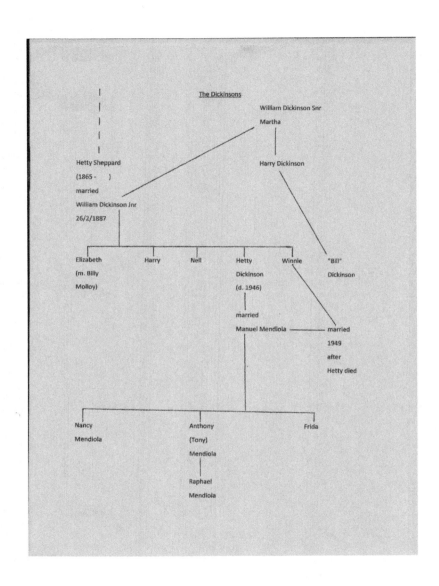

The Dickinsons

William Dickinson Snr
Martha

Hetty Sheppard
(1865 -   )
married
William Dickinson Jnr
26/2/1887

Harry Dickinson

Elizabeth   Harry   Nell   Hetty   Winnie   "Bill"
(m. Billy   Dickinson   Dickinson
Molloy)   (d. 1946)

married

Manuel Mendiola ———— married
                              1949
                              after
                              Hetty died

Nancy   Anthony   Frida
Mendiola   (Tony)
                         Mendiola

                         Raphael
                         Mendiola

158

III.

Who

Killed

Bessie Sheppard?

A couple of items in the Nottingham papers of 1817, buried within the trivia of county life, caught my eye. Together they told in no great detail of the inauguration in Mansfield of a clandestine society of local businessmen. They based themselves at the Crown and Anchor Inn, long since demolished but at that time situated in the street somewhat inelegantly called Spittlehouse Gate, at the lower end of Nottingham Road in the town centre. They were called the Oddfellows. The base they had created for themselves at the Inn they named *Number 10 - Minerva*. No names of members were reported but the article did mention that local curiosity was aroused to such an extent by the formation of the society that a large crowd gathered outside the Crown and Anchor to witness what was described as a mysterious event, an event shrouded in talk of passwords and secret rituals.

I had come across the Oddfellows before, but my interest was confined to mild amusement at their choice of name. It was now, however, freshly aroused. The ceremony described had taken place just seven weeks after the murder of Bess. They are variously described as *members of a fraternity similar to the Freemasons* and *members of a secret society established for mutual aid and social enjoyment.* The *social enjoyment* I could readily understand; even the *mutual aid* had, conceivably, an air of innocence about it for they assisted as part of their *raison d'etre* to help workers not covered by the auspices of other guilds. But why the secrecy? What would they wish to contain with their secrecy?

They were listed in the phone book, so I rang their local number. A man called Lane told me that the Mansfield *lodge*, as he referred to it, was called The Rising Star and was inaugurated in 1832. But this was fifteen years after *Minerva*, of which he said he had never heard. I asked him about the secrecy of the Oddfellows and the rituals involved

161

in their meetings. He sounded a little uncomfortable, not because there was anything to hide, but because he was embarrassed. The clandestine nature of the Oddfellows, he assured me, was a thing of the past. The order had grown up. It had come of age.

Its foundations, he went on to explain, were laid down long ago by the itinerant craftsmen, the skilled journeymen who, needing places to stay, organised a network of safe houses or *lodges*. For a small fee artisan travellers could enjoy within these lodges a tolerable degree of comfort for the duration of their stay in any locality. Early on the Oddfellows split into two separate factions or orders, the Ancient Order and the Patriotic Order. Both were politically motivated, the one supporting the Whigs, the other the Tories. In 1779 these two merged and became the supposedly apolitical Union Order. The lodge system thrived but, with an increasing number of members calling upon their services, a financial strain was felt by the smaller ones. This strain led, in 1810, to the formation of what was known as the Manchester Unity, which came to see itself as the dominant body.

Lane went on to tell me that, though some backing was given to the lodges with the formation of the Manchester Unity, many tended to go their own way, clinging to their political allegiances and their old, now outdated, rituals. Control of these was minimal. He advised me to contact the Nottingham Oddfellows in order to trace *Minerva*. Though they, too, were of no real help, they did acknowledge that it was probably one of their original lodges which blossomed and died with alarming regularity. Such records as were kept by them were, at best, poor, at worst, non-existent.

The history related to me by Lane sounded familiar. In essence, it paralleled that of the Freemasons and I wondered to what extent the two organisations may have shared common roots. Both, I knew, had become influential in

America. If the Oddfellows freely borrowed their rituals and regalia from the senior order (which they did according to Lane - he described it as poor man's Freemasonry) to what extent did they freely borrow their history too?

Back in the 12th and 13th centuries, during the great era of cathedral construction, skilled stonemasons would travel the land plying their trade wherever they were needed. Lodges were inaugurated in exactly the same manner as Lane had described to me those of the Oddfellows. Because of the spread of the masons across the land they needed to be able to recognise one another in order to prevent interlopers stealing both their livelihoods and their hospitality. To this end they devised, for purely practical reasons, an elaborate system of codes, handshakes and ritual greetings. With the passing of the grand Gothic period of construction the itinerant nature of the masons' work diminished and the rituals fell to disuse. The clandestine structure, however, remained.

In the late 17th and early 18th centuries the masonic rituals were resurrected by the upper classes and aristocracy. Somehow the concept of male exclusivity and the aura of secrecy appealed to their conceit. Modern masonry was born. The lodges were revived, not now for any practical reason, but as social centres for the new breed of soft-palmed *free*mason - those not tied to the mason's traditional trade. With extraordinary zeal they set about reinventing their own history and imbuing it with a sense of their own importance, linking it back to the days of Solomon and the Tower of Babel. In some instances lineage was claimed even back to Adam himself. The Christian emphasis, so much part of the original masonic creed, was eradicated to such an extent that they even began to measure time, not from the birth of Christ - AD, but from the Advent of the Light - AL. The advent of the light, it seemed, predated the birth of Christ by some four thousand and four years -

163

putting them effectively in the same bed as Creationists - and present day Freemasons may still refer to 2014AD as 6018AL.

So, was there some mongrelisation of the histories of Freemasonry and Oddfellowship? They certainly tallied fairly closely. Whatever the truth, both appear to have given way to a more hedonistic philosophy than that in place at their inception. They were social gatherings for the benefit, not primarily, of travellers, but for that of the local, static business community. Poor man's Freemasonry seems, on the whole, an apt description of Oddfellowship.

Today the Oddfellows is a wholly respectable grouping of financial organisations, no more guilty of harbouring sinister secrets than any other, though in this post financial crisis era, I hasten to add, that's not really saying a lot. The Nottingham group disbanded its lodges in the 1940s with such names as *Temple of Justice* and *Wild Man* being lost forever. Their prime function, even in the early days, was to provide help for those of their number who fell on hard times. I daresay that for the most part they were loyal to that function. There persists, however, a certain unease born of their secrecy. Clues regarding their ethos may well lie in press reports of a more recent origin to those hitherto considered in this enquiry. The Mansfield Chronicle, the local newspaper, in November 1932 said of the Oddfellows when reporting on one of its celebratory dinners:

It started as a gathering of men who met once a week for an evening's conviviality. Occasionally one would be absent and the others, on enquiring about him, would learn that he was sick or injured, or otherwise unable to follow his employment. They would say, "We must help him."

This brief account of the origins of Oddfellowship makes no mention of its sense of duty toward the artisan as being the prime motive for its formation. On the contrary, it

164

implies that its original function had been *for an evening's conviviality*, and that any social aspect was a consequence of a member missing the evening's carousing. A second, earlier report in the same newspaper following yet another dinner in November 1908 attributes the following to one of the Grand Masters (another term shared with Freemasonry) who addressed the diners:

Every brother had to pay proper respect to the officers of the lodge and in that way he learned to pay respect to those in authority in other places. They also learned to conduct public business, and they were glad to observe that members of the Unity and kindred associations had been exalted to public positions in connection with the towns in which they lived.

Perhaps it is symptomatic of the modern age that one reads the above with a certain cynicism. Clearly those embraced by the Oddfellows, those willing to pay the *proper respect*, had the potential to prosper. Whether that is still the case today I have no idea, but back then, in the days of the Regency - a hundred years before the 1908 speech - what were they really like? In what circumstances would the desire to help a brother apply? Would it matter what the nature of the trouble was that the brother found himself in?

It seems to me unlikely that the Mansfield Oddfellows who convened at the Crown and Anchor Inn in September 1817 would not have included within their number the very same men who had patronised the coffee room in the Swan Inn, just round the corner. Was it not inevitable that such a secret order would attract those who judged themselves to be important? Big fish in, albeit, a small parochial pond? Could any of the businessmen of Mansfield afford *not* to seek membership, realising as they must, what the commercial consequences might be of exclusion?

Secret societies, though perhaps formed with the most honourable of intent do, by virtue of their very secrecy, attract those who potentially have the more secrets to protect. The creed of loyalty, though initially untested, will inevitably be invoked to suppress that which, under different circumstances, individual members might deem dishonourable. The instinct of the herd to survive and to offer safe harbour to those among its number, I believe, could have played a significant part in this story.

***

Curious as to the origins of the name of the lodge, I dipped into Greek and Roman mythology. Minerva, to the Greeks, was the very same goddess as was Athene to the Romans. She was goddess of handicrafts and weavers, artists and actors. Mansfield's location at the heart of the Nottinghamshire textile region seemed to explain the derivation adequately. However, before I closed the book, I came across an odd coincidence.

Athene was the daughter of Zeus. When Zeus discovered that his wife Metis was pregnant he was fearful lest the birth of a son usurp his powers. Zeus solved the problem, as you would, by eating his wife whole. Beset by terrible headaches and screaming to the heavens, he was overheard by Hermes who understood the source of his pain - the infant within his consumed wife was demanding birth. Hermes instructed Hephaestus to cure Zeus' pain by bringing about the birth of the child. The somewhat unorthodox obstetric technique employed by Hephaestus - long fallen from the midwifery protocol - was to cleave open Zeus' head with an axe. From his gaping skull emerged the child Athene - or Minerva as the Romans would have it.

Was I becoming over-sensitized or did the emergence of the infant Minerva from the split skull of Zeus, in some

166

eerie way, echo the fate of Bessie Sheppard and the *birth*, some seven weeks later, of the Oddfellows lodge, *Minerva*?

***

The Mansfield Directory of 1832 lists the names of those men who owned quarries. Half were also stonemasons - the very men I would have expected to be drawn to the infant Oddfellows prior to the founding of any masonic order proper in Mansfield. Among their number in 1817 was a young man in his twenties called Anthony Buckles. In April that year Anthony Buckles took himself a wife, Ann. The union, unfortunately, was childless. Buckles had premises on the Cockpit, a stretch of what is now the beginning of the Nottingham Road. Close by was the Crown and Anchor and beyond, Spittlehouse Gate. Anthony Buckles was the only man ever named in connection with the raising of the memorial stone to Bess. The rest are referred to in a way that echoes much of what I had learned of both the Sheppard's benefactors and the membership of the Swan Coffee House and the Oddfellows as the *gentlemen of Mansfield.*

The *gentlemen* Buckles had organised to raise the stone, the *gentlemen* responsible for the charity concert and the *gentlemen* who founded *Minerva* just seven weeks after Bess' murder, had to be, either in whole or part, the same individuals. Could these *gentlemen,* whether in the guise of *Minerva* or whatever, have been connected with her death if Charles Rotherham was, indeed, innocent? But what did it prove? Perhaps they were just genuinely compassionate.

I already had quite real doubts about the guilt of Charles Rotherham. If he was innocent, someone else was guilty. After all this time I could hardly expect the real culprit to emerge from the woodwork, hands raised in surrender, clutching some metaphorical smoking gun. I had to search

167

through whatever was available, whatever I had been able to discover or deduce, to see if there was a credible alternative explanation for the events of July and August of 1817. I suspected that a plausible answer was staring me in the face, but it was one which gave me little or no comfort. This answer was luring me down a path whose course would compel me to cast doubt upon the morality of not just one man, the real murderer. It would cast doubt on Regency Mansfield itself.

***

Compassion alone failed to be an adequate response to the questions that had dogged me for so long.

Why did Benjamin Barnes pursue Rotherham to the exclusion of all other lines of enquiry?

Why did the affluent gentlemen of Mansfield show such charity - a charity I could not find replicated for one of their own - to a stranger?

Why did the stone on the Nottingham Road bear not the name of Elizabeth Sheppard alone, but also, for all time, the name of the man hanged for her murder?

I was uncomfortable with the conclusion towards which I was reluctantly, but inexorably, drawn. That the activities of *Minerva* were somehow connected with her death.

Elizabeth Sheppard, it is said, left her home in Papplewick to look for work. She was, we are told, successful; she found work. Nowhere - and this is surely unusual bearing in mind the circumstances - nowhere are we told just *where* she obtained work. I already doubted that it would have been in the mills of Mansfield because of the preponderance of similar opportunities in Papplewick and the reputation mill work had earned for itself under Robinson with the mass graves of orphans as testimony to

168

his neglect. The coaching inns of Mansfield, notably the Swan, were a likely alternative. But would Bess working in the inns explain the display of sympathy exhibited on her death? It would certainly give her increased opportunity for acquaintance with the Mansfield folk than would mill work, would it not? But then, are we not told that she had only just found this work on the 7th? Was that not the whole point of the trip to Mansfield? Had she worked in the inn at all, it could have been for no more than a few hours. Scarcely sufficient time to forge the bonds that would account for the powerful wave of compassion that overwhelmed the town and that persisted through to the erection of the monument some years later. There had to be something else.

There was but one answer, loath as I was to contemplate it. That answer would explain why the story that she had gone to Mansfield to seek work had emerged and why it had been allowed, down the years, to prevail. It would explain, too, why Mary Sheppard allowed the myths surrounding Bess to be perpetuated and why she never, in return for the charity extended to her, mentioned her daughter's real purpose in Mansfield. It would explain both her being well known and why this had to be concealed.

Far from being a stranger in town, Elizabeth Sheppard was, on the contrary, perhaps a frequent visitor. She had gone to town that day not to *find* work, but to *continue* it. Elizabeth Sheppard may well have been a prostitute.

***

The Mansfield of 1817 was no idyllic corner of a green and pleasant land that both local history books and Jane Austen would have us believe England to have been. It was a dirty, dangerous place. Poverty and near starvation were endemic. To deny these unpalatable truths is to deny our own history, our reality. Girls could make a living with their bodies off the fine Regency gentlemen, the Regency

169

gentlemen who would slake their appetites in the flash houses. How convenient for them to be able to ease the tedium of their long coach journeys in the arms of a young girl at one of the coaching inns en route.

Prostitution did not then, nor does it now, carry with it any necessarily moral compromise. Often for the practitioner there is no alternative and it is resorted to for the purest of motives. When needs must, so often is the devil at the wheel. Bess knew that, if all else failed, she could make a living off the clientele in the coaching inns. She was a resolute, determined girl. With no father to provide for the family she would set aside all dignity - who, indeed, could afford such a luxury - and do what she had to put food on the table of her mother and little brother.

How would this perception of Bess fit the pattern? Mary was aware of the true nature of her daughter's business in Mansfield - surely, if I'm right, she had to have been - and it would certainly account for her worries regarding her safety. Would not Bess' prostitution go a long way toward explaining the response of the gentlemen of Mansfield on hearing of her death? Aware, as they no doubt were, that she was the sole breadwinner in the Sheppard home, is there not now sense in their understanding of Mary's urgent need for money? Is not their heartwarming display of charity more understandable? But would this answer all the questions?

The men of Mansfield, specifically the men of *Minerva*, would be anxious that the truth was not discovered. Untold damage could be wreaked upon reputations, businesses, families and their standing in the community if the true nature of their *conviviality* became known. Could not the efforts made by these men to suppress the truth, to keep their secret, go some way to accounting for the dearth of information about Bess that I first encountered?

Convincing as I believe it sounds, it does not yet fully explain the necessity for Charles Rotherham's arrest and rapid hanging. Was there still a yet greater secret hidden behind the doors of *Minerva?*

***

The possibility that Bessie Sheppard was a prostitute explains many of the paradoxes in the sketchy story that has been handed down over the years. The scattered, incomprehensible pieces of the jigsaw were, near two hundred years later, beginning to fit neatly, and disturbingly, into place. The picture emerging was one of greater complexity and sadness than I had imagined. One corner of the jigsaw, however, remained incomplete. Perhaps, within the box, I had the pieces that could finish it.

That Bess died the victim of a violent and irrational act of unexplained spontaneity now was in my mind in doubt. That she died in some way as a consequence of her profession now seemed increasingly possible.. Until now I had been unable to work out just why Ben Barnes had directed all his energies toward catching up with Charles Rotherham. It seemed clear now that he was perhaps pointed in that direction by someone on the morning of the 8th of July, the day the body was found. That someone, I believe, was a member of the Coffee House group and subsequently the Oddfellows lodge, *Minerva,* inaugurated just seven weeks later at the Crown and Anchor, He did what he did that morning out of a sense of loyalty. He had taken an oath of allegiance and secrecy. He did what he did because the real killer of Bessie Sheppard was also a member of the incipient *Minerva.*

The lodge could not have materialised overnight. Men do not embrace bonds of mutual trust and reliance unless those bonds already exist in embryonic form. *Minerva,* with its roots firmly fixed in the group of elite gentlemen who

171

convened each week at the Swan, clearly had to have been thus when Bess died. Bad enough that among their secrets was the fact that they consorted with prostitutes, worse still that they included the murder that led to the birth of *Minerva*, all underscored by their oaths of allegiance.

It was essential then that Barnes be diverted away from Mansfield. Too much could be discovered were he to be allowed to go there. He had to be sent, at all costs, to Nottingham, away from the truth, in pursuit of a stranger. What better motivation to ensure gentlemanly unity in the concealment of a murderer - a notion no doubt odious to many among them - than the sure and certain knowledge that the exposure of the culprit would lead inevitably to the disclosure of their own transgressions? The bonds that were to link members of *Minerva* had less to do with brotherly love and much more with brotherly fear.

How then could they take control of the investigation? How could they effectively divert attention away from themselves? They needed a scapegoat. Someone upon whom they could convincingly pin the blame for Bess' death. Someone unlikely to attract sympathy on his arrest. But who? Is it not possible that, through their very own traveller's lodge, the ideal candidate had passed? A man seeking work? That scissorsmith? The ex-soldier? Had this man not been well on the way to oblivion when they last saw him? Who would question *his* guilt? Who would stand up for *him*? Wouldn't it be assumed when he denied it - if they ever caught him, wasn't he long gone by now? - that he'd killed her in a drunken frenzy? What was his name? Rotherham? That was it. Charles Rotherham.

On the morning of the 8th of July the body of Elizabeth Sheppard was found by John Womley, the quarryman. Anthony Buckles was a quarry owner and a mason. As the man nominally responsible for the erection of the stone on the highway, he was likely to have been a member of

Minerva. Is it possible, in view of what I now suggest might have been the truth about Bess, that Womley either knew her or, by reputation, knew *of* her? There were some three hours unaccounted for between Womley having his suspicions aroused that morning and his actually reporting that he had found a body. Could Womley, during this time, have informed whoever he believed had an interest in hearing of the death - Buckles, perhaps - *in advance of notifying the authorities*? Could someone have been despatched to the scene, ostensibly to begin enquiries? We know that by the time Barnes arrived lawyer Walkden and Colonel Need, two *members of the nobility and gentry*, were present at the scene. Could they too have been nascent members of *Minerva*? Were they not the ideal men to convince Ben Barnes of the stranger's existence and send him off, away from Mansfield?

Perhaps certain men of *Minerva* knew of the murder before the body was even discovered. Perhaps they learned of it on the evening of the 7th from the lips of the murderer himself? Could they, behind the locked door of the Swan or the Crown and Anchor, have formulated a plan to conceal the murderer and their involvement in the dead girl's life from the rest of the town? Of course, they would have to ensure that Mary Sheppard remained silent. It would cost them, but then, what was the alternative?

***

So who killed Bessie Sheppard? And why? Did her death occur spontaneously due to the combination of drink and lust. Or was it, perhaps, premeditated? Did she die on the road, or was she deposited there having been killed elsewhere? Was she, perhaps, pregnant and had come to Mansfield to seek money from whoever she believed was the father in return for her silence? She is described in one of the first news reports I ever read on the case as

173

interesting. One old definition of this is, in fact, pregnant. Perhaps Anthony Buckles himself killed her and his own childless marriage was poetic justice. We will, I regret, never really know.

Bess died, as did Charles Rotherham, a victim of the times. Poverty, unemployment, ignorance and prejudice then, as they still do now, conspired to change the pattern of their lives. Corruption and immorality perhaps conspired to silence them after death.

The *gentlemen* were never questioned about any involvement. Their outpourings of charity and compassion have been accepted by generations as genuine. The man adjudged to be responsible for Bess' death was hanged. They made absolutely certain we never forgot. In an act of deep compassion and humanity they etched his name upon her memorial.

As for Ben Barnes; was he stupid, corrupt or simply complicit? Well, he went on to be Governor of the Nottingham Workhouse. Was this reward for his complicity?

His partner, Linneker, never made such progress. He never testified against Rotherham. In 1832 he was still a humble police constable living on Greyhound Yard, Nottingham.

Further developments

I've brought out this second edition of The Murder of Bessie Sheppard both to add the footnote that follows regarding later events and also to compact the original, thereby bringing down the costs and therefore the price. From now on the book will be available at the lowest price possible with no profit margin in it for me. It will be at cost price. Can't however, do anything about delivery charges.

The book originally came out in January of 2015, just two and a half years ago. I'd had this obsession for as long as I could remember but, the thing was, it didn't stop there. Almost immediately my wife, Chris, began to search for more descendants. I was quite happy with that, I believed my obsession was largely cured. How *wrong* I was.

Within a very short time she came up with extra details of Richard Sheppard, Joseph's son and Bess' nephew. Soon after, she found an aerial photograph of where he used to live in Mansfield - I know, not just a photograph, a damned *aerial* photograph.

One evening she went quiet; it's never a good sign. What she was up to was contacting this man in California named Rafael Mendiola, who, as luck would have it - her *luck;* it would never be my luck - turned out to be the son of my old pen pal, Anthony (Tony) Mendiola, with whom I had corresponded in Lima, Peru. Rafael, or Rafi as we now know him, is a teacher in Bakersfield, California. Through him I was lucky enough to make contact with other members of the Mendiola family in Peru, notably the gorgeous Cristina and her children - all descendants of Joseph Sheppard, the brother of Bess.

I renewed contact with Richard Morley, the stonemason I had met years before who was largely influenced in his final career choice by the story of Bess, and, following a search of records, we located the unmarked grave of the tragic, but enormously courageous, Richard Sheppard. Thanks to Richard Morley and the kind folk who run Mansfield cemetery, Richard Sheppard now has a headstone, fashioned and put in place by the other Richard.

As a strange coincidence, the very first time I stood beside the grave of Richard Sheppard, at that time unmarked and overgrown with a sprawling rhododendron, it was precisely one hundred years *to the day* after his death. I believe in very little, but that made me jump!

I'm more than pleased to report that the family traces and links we've established resulted in June of this year in the first visit to the graveside of their hitherto unknown ancestor, Richard Sheppard, of the wonderfully effervescent Vanessa from Peru and the Zumba-loving, gorgeous Maria Laura from Gothenburg, Sweden, where she, also a Peruvian, now lives with her Swedish husband and family. Both were given the full, conducted tour by Chris, my wife, (to whom I'm eternally grateful, being socially inept myself) of all the locations in the book.

It was a long, long quest on my part to discover what I could of Bessie Sheppard and Charles Rotherham and, though the first leg of that quest was somewhat long-winded, this second stage since the book came out has been, at times both frenetic and wonderful. My wife and I are now friends with folk whom we would never have known other than through Bess. For that I thank her. She's precious to me - she always will be. I just hope that between us, we've done her proud and that her existence is a soft and gentle presence in all our minds. At last she has her folks.

David Marshall

October 2017

Epilogue (to First Edition)

When I first learned of the murder of Bessie Sheppard in 1972 I was a long-haired, directionless lad of twenty-five; an extremely junior civil servant with a wife, two children and no money.

Today, with this book finally complete, I'm sixty-seven, married to my second unfortunate wife and still broke.

I had no aims at the outset other than to satisfy my curiosity. They developed as my involvement with Bessie Sheppard grew. Over the years I became swept up in the sheer sadness of it all. Gradually it came to occupy a vast, unexpected chunk of my life.

The two central characters, Bessie Sheppard and Charles Rotherham, were real people, unfortunately remembered now solely for having both come to violent ends. That seemed harsh. Unfair.

No matter who they are nor what they have done, everyone deserves that someone speak up on their behalf. This I hope I've done for Charles Rotherham. Everyone, too, deserves to be carried in a family's memory. Finding Tony Mendiola in far off Peru, I hope I've achieved that for Bess.

Of course, I've conclusively proven nothing; it was always far too late for that. But I hope that what I have been able to do is to sow the seed of doubt in your mind and, perhaps even at this late date, served the interests of justice. We can bring none of our characters back. We must, however, remember them as more than just names carved into a block of stone.

DWM 2014 (First Edition)

The author in Norfolk with his greyhounds,

Jake and Annie.

(This and front cover photograph by Chris Marshall)

Please note, for anyone wishing to read more and see photographs of Bess' Peruvian and American descendants, there is a Facebook page called The Murder of Bessie Sheppard. Please feel free to join.

.

.

Printed in Great Britain
by Amazon